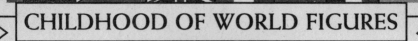

CHILDHOOD OF WORLD FIGURES

POPE JOHN PAUL II

YOUNG MAN OF THE CHURCH

By George E. Stanley

D0191305

Aladdin Paperbacks
New York   London   Toronto   Sydney

To Dr. Andrea Marie Montgomery,
our daughter-in-law-to-be!

☙ALADDIN PAPERBACKS
An imprint of Simon & Schuster Children's Publishing Division
1230 Avenue of the Americas, New York, NY 10020
Text copyright © 2005 by George E. Stanley
All rights reserved, including the right of reproduction in whole or in part in any form.
ALADDIN PAPERBACKS, CHILDHOOD OF WORLD FIGURES, and colophon are trademarks of Simon & Schuster, Inc.
Designed by Lisa Vega
The text of this book was set in Aldine721 BT.
Manufactured in the United States of America
First Aladdin Paperbacks edition July 2005
10 9 8 7 6 5 4 3 2 1
Library of Congress Control Number 2005926077
ISBN 1-4169-1282-7

CONTENTS

POPE JOHN PAUL II

CHAPTER ONE
CHILD OF A FREE POLAND

At the sound of his mother's cries from the bedroom, thirteen-year-old Edmund Wojtyla—known in the family as "Mundek"—turned to his father and said, "Will Mama be all right?"

Lieutenant Karol Wojtyla smiled. "Of course, Mundek," he said. "Childbirth is a natural thing, and the midwife has delivered hundreds of children here in Wadowice."

"I hope it's a boy," Mundek said. He grinned at his father. "I would like very much to have a brother who might one day grow up to be the pope."

Mundek saw a shadow pass across his father's face, and he suddenly wished now that he had thought before he had spoken. His parents were probably wanting a daughter to fill the emptiness left by his sister, Olga, who had only lived for a few days. Mundek vaguely remembered their baptizing the tiny girl at home, something he knew the church permitted in emergencies, and then, within hours, burying her in an unmarked grave in Wadowice's cemetery. After that, his parents never mentioned Olga again.

"I don't think that will ever happen, Mundek," Lieutenant Wojtyla said. "Popes don't come from Poland."

Another cry from the tiny bedroom sent Karol to the door. He opened it slightly, just enough to peer inside, and said, "Good midwife, do you need anything?"

"Yes! I need for you to pull your head back from that door and close it!" the midwife hissed at him. "This is no time for a man to be present!"

As her husband shut the door without comment, Emilia Wojtyla wondered if she would survive this birth. She had no strength left.

"You're doing fine, Mrs. Wojtyla," the midwife said soothingly. "The child is taking its time, but there are no complications."

Emilia took a deep breath and let it out. "Do I hear singing?" she asked, her voice barely above a whisper.

"Yes, Mrs. Wojtyla, you do," the midwife said.

"Why?" Emilia asked.

"The people of Wadowice are celebrating, Mrs. Wojtyla. This is May 18, 1920, a date that we will never forget," the midwife said. She looked at the clock on the wall. "Marshal Pilsudski's train has probably arrived at the station."

Even as another pain shot through her body, Emilia managed to smile. "Oh yes, how could I have forgotten?" she said. "My child will be born into a free Poland."

In April, Marshal Józef Pilsudski had signed an alliance with Ukraine's Symon Petliura to wage a joint war against the Soviet Union. Under Pilsudski's command the Polish and Ukrainian armies launched a successful offensive against the Russian troops in

Ukraine. On May 7 they won a major victory when they captured the Ukrainian city Kiev.

Outside, the singing and shouting grew. The midwife went to the window.

"What do you see?" Emilia asked.

"I see many, many people," the midwife replied. "I see a horse-drawn carriage covered in flowers, and inside it, Marshal Pilsudski is waving to everyone."

"Open the window, please," Emilia said.

The midwife did as she was asked, and the bedroom was suddenly flooded with light.

Emilia let out a sharp cry, and the midwife returned to her side. Within minutes, the midwife had delivered the baby.

"It's a boy, Mrs. Wojtyla," the midwife proclaimed, just as the bells summoning people to prayer began from St. Mary's Church across the street.

On June 20, Emilia, still weak but beaming with pride, surrounded by her husband and Mundek and a few friends, held her new son in her arms while a military chaplain, Father Franciszek Zak, baptized the baby.

When Father Zak asked, "What name will you give this child?" Karol said, in a strong voice, Karol Józef Wojtyla.

It was Emilia who had insisted that the boy be given his father's first name, but for Karol, there had never been any question as to what his son's middle name would be. Józef would honor not only Marshal Pilsudski, the founding hero of the newly independent Polish Republic, but also Franz Józef, emperor of Austria-Hungary from 1848 to 1916, in whose army Karol had proudly served.

As the weeks passed, the baby, whom the family now called Lolek, surprised everyone by gaining more weight than had been expected; the midwife had been concerned that because Emilia was so weak, her milk wouldn't be nourishing enough. Friends who visited the Wojtylas remarked that Lolek was the picture of good health.

Soon Emilia, too, had regained enough of her strength that she was able to get out of bed and resume some of her normal activities.

"Are you sure you shouldn't rest for a few more days?" Karol asked her. "Mundek and I can take care of ourselves and Lolek, too, except when he's nursing."

"I'm fine, Karol," Emilia told her husband. "I don't want to be waited on anymore."

At first, Emilia would only be out of bed for an hour or so before she began to tire, but gradually she stayed up longer and longer, and one day she announced, "I'm taking Lolek for a stroll in his pram."

"It's a beautiful day for that, Mama," Mundek said. "You'll enjoy the flowers and the trees in the park."

"But if you get too tired, Emilia, you should sit on one of the benches," Karol said. "Lolek can watch the children play." He pinched Lolek's cheek. "At this rate, he'll be joining them before long."

"Yes, I'd like very much to see the park,

because I've already missed the first blooms of this year," Emilia said, "but I'm also going to pay a visit to the photographer."

As Mundek carried the pram down the steps of their second-floor apartment at Rynek, 2, he met Chaim Blamuth, the owner of the building, coming up the steps.

"Good morning, Mr. Blamuth," Mundek said. "How are you?"

"I'll know more after I talk to your father, Mundek," Mr. Blamuth said.

Mundek continued on down the steps and out onto the street. Mr. Blamuth was an honest landlord, Mundek believed, but he was a Jew, and he was always wanting to talk about the political events in Poland and what effects they might have on the Jewish people. Because of Lieutenant Wotyla's military background, Mr. Blamuth had a lot of faith in what Mundek's father believed was happening in the country. After the joy of May, the summer had brought dread to the nation, and several times of late, Mundek had overheard his father whispering to his mother that Polish history might soon repeat itself and the country would no longer be an independent state.

The Red Cavalry of General Semën Budënnyi was at that very moment moving westward from Ukraine toward Germany. Unfortunately, as Mundek and everyone else knew too well, Poland was in its way. The country would be trampled by the godless Communists, the new rulers of Russia, with no regard whatsoever.

Mundek set the pram down on the sidewalk and leaned up against the building, enjoying the warmth that soaked through the back of his shirt. He thought about how what was happening to Poland now would affect him and his family. In just a few years he planned to enter Jagiellonian University in Kraków to study medicine. Would the Russians put an end to his dreams? he wondered.

"Thank you, Mundek," Emilia said. "You're a good son."

"I'll walk with you, if you want, Mother,"

Mundek said. He took Lolek from his mother's arms and put him in the pram. "I can push it, while you—"

"I shall be fine, Mundek," Emilia said, interrupting him. "Why don't you go over to the soccer field and see if there's a game you can join? You've not had very much exercise these past few weeks. I'm getting stronger each day, and you no longer need to be so concerned about me."

"Well, if you're sure you'll be all right," Mundek said.

Emilia kissed him lightly on the cheek. "Yes, I'm sure, dear," she said.

Emilia watched as Mundek headed in the opposite direction. He was such a handsome young man. She could only imagine what the future held for him. One of these days, she was sure, Mundek would be Poland's most famous doctor. He'd live in a large house in Warsaw and treat all the important people in Poland. She had no doubt of that whatsoever.

Emilia began pushing the pram down the

sidewalk. As she knew they would, everyone stopped her to comment on what a beautiful baby Lolek was. With each compliment, Emilia's heart swelled with pride.

It was only when she finally reached the park that Emily realized how tired she was, so she sat on a bench under a tree and, turning the pram so that Lolek could watch the other children at play, leaned back and closed her eyes for a few minutes.

"Mrs. Wojtyla?" a woman's voice said.

Emilia opened her eyes. The sun was behind the person's head, so her face was in darkness. Emilia shaded her eyes to see who had spoken to her.

"Mrs. Sikorski! What a pleasure!" Emilia said as her eyes focused to recognize the butcher's wife. "It's so nice to see you."

"Are you all right?" Mrs. Sikorski asked.

"Oh, yes," Emilia said. "Lolek and I were just enjoying some sun."

Mrs. Sikorski reached down and chucked Lolek under the chin. "He's such a *healthy* child," she said. Looking up quickly at Emilia, she added, "Oh, I'm sorry, I didn't mean to imply anything."

"It's all right, Mrs. Sikorski," Emilia said. "I've not been well these last few years, and I, too, was quite concerned that Lolek would be affected in some way by my health, but as you can see, he's quite all right."

"Yes, yes, he is," Mrs. Sikorski said. "You must be very proud of him."

"Oh yes, we are, Mrs. Sikorski," Emilia said. "One day, our Lolek will be a great man."

Mrs. Sikorski pinched one of Lolek's cheeks. "It certainly doesn't hurt that he has that good, broad Slavic face that we Poles prize so highly." She looked up at Emilia. "I am on my way to the church to light a candle for my nephew, who's on the front with Marshal Pilsudski. I shall add Lolek to my prayers, that he can grow up in an independent Poland, but I'm afraid that the news isn't good today." She looked around, then leaned down next to Emilia's ear and whispered, "My husband has heard that when the Red Army retakes Poland, a Provisional Polish Revolutionary Committee will be set up to run the country." She stood up and added, again in a whisper, "It will be headed by Feliks Dzerzhínskii. Of course you know who he is, don't you?"

Emilia shook her head. Actually, she had heard the name from her husband, but right now she was too tired to listen to anymore of Mrs. Sikorski's conversation about what was happening in their part of Europe. "I don't pay much attention to politics, Mrs. Sikorski," she said. "I leave that to my husband."

"You should, Mrs. Wojtyla. Your family's existence could depend on it," Mrs. Sikorski said. "Dzerzhínskii is the head of the Cheka, the Soviet Secret Police. He's the most feared man in the Soviet Union."

Suddenly, Emily shivered, but she knew it wasn't because the sun was now hidden by a cloud. She grasped the arm of the bench to help her stand up. "I should be going," she said. "I'm on my way to the photographer's to have a picture taken of Lolek and me."

"I must see it when it's ready," Mrs. Sikorski said.

"I'll be happy to show it to you," Emilia said.

For a few minutes after Mrs. Sikorski had left, Emily remained with the backs of her legs propped up against the bench to keep from falling. She felt dizzy and even a little nauseated and was frightened, although she didn't know if it was because of her physical condition or because of her encounter with Mrs. Sikorski. She wished now that she had let Mundek come with her. If she fainted here, she could only hope that whoever found her would go fetch Karol to help her, but after a few minutes, and several deep breaths of the fresh air, she was feeling better.

At first, Emilia considered putting off her trip to the photographer's and returning to the apartment, but she was suddenly afraid that something might happen to keep her from ever having her picture taken with Lolek, so she willed herself to push the pram through the park and to the photographer's studio.

Two weeks later, on August 18, the photograph was ready, but it was Karol who went to get it. He also purchased a dark wooden frame and asked the photographer to wrap it in bright paper and tie it with a red ribbon. Emilia had just awakened from a nap when Karol returned. He handed the package to her.

"What is this?" Emilia asked.

Karol smiled. "Open it and find out," he said.

As Emilia pulled back the last piece of the wrapping paper, she and Lolek were looking back at her. "Oh, Karol," she said. "It turned out perfect, didn't it?"

"Yes, it did," Karol said. "Lolek is his mother's child. You can easily see the resemblance between you two."

Emilia hugged the frame. "I shall treasure this always," she said.

Just then, there was a heavy knocking on

the front door of the apartment. It continued until Karol opened it, revealing a flushed and agitated Chaim Blamuth.

"Is something wrong, Mr. Blamuth?" Karol asked.

"Have you not heard the wonderful news?" Mr. Blamuth blurted out. "Marshal Pilsudski has defeated the Red Army!"

"No, no, I hadn't heard that!" Karol said. He stepped aside. "Please come in, Mr. Blamuth, and tell us everything you know."

Mr. Blamuth, who always enjoyed being the center of attention, had managed to telephone a cousin in Warsaw, who gave him the news of events that no one else in Wadowice knew. He was hurrying from friend to friend in the town to make sure that everyone realized he was the first one to know the information.

With the Red Army almost in Warsaw, a Polish delegation had left for Minsk, where they hoped to start negotiations for a surrender. They knew that Dzerzhínskii was not far from Warsaw. Marshall Pilsudski, though, was not prepared to concede defeat. In a daring move, he secretly redeployed some of his best divisions to the Vistula River to take advantage of weaknesses in the Soviet Army, which had begun to attack Warsaw. By the night of August 17, the Red Army had been reduced to a rabble of fleeing refugees.

"Poland is saved!" Mr. Blamuth shouted. "Poland is still free."

Just then, Lolek, who had been sleeping in Emilia's arms, opened his eyes.

"Oh, I'm sorry, Mrs. Wojtyla, I didn't mean to awaken the child," Mr. Blamuth whispered.

Emilia smiled at him. "Oh, please don't apologize, Mr. Blamuth," she said. "This is something that Lolek needed to hear."

CHAPTER TWO

THE WORLD OUTSIDE THE WINDOW

Lolek pulled up a chair next to an earthenware urn that was just inside the doorway of the apartment and sat down to wait for his seventeen-year-old brother, Mundek. Although Lolek's fourth birthday was not for two more days, Mundek had told him that morning, before he left for school, that when he got home, he was going to give Lolek his birthday present. He was going to show Lolek everything there was to see in Wadowice.

Until now, and for as long as he could remember, Lolek had been content with trips to the nearby park with his mother, or with his entire family to St. Mary's Church for Mass, or sometimes with his father to draw water from wells in the market square for drinking and bathing, but now, Mundek had said, Lolek would go places he had never been before.

Lolek had often sat at the windows of the apartment on days when his mother wasn't feeling well, watching the scenes below him: the horse-drawn carriages; the people walking— and, once in a while, a loud object that his mother said was called an automobile. It had never occurred to Lolek that he could go other places too, that he could actually be a part of what was taking place in Wadowice. His mother had never mentioned that to him before. Now, he wondered why. Lolek had just assumed that for the rest of his life he would only *watch* the world from the windows of their apartment.

Lolek had never minded it, though. To him, being in their apartment always gave him the same warm feeling he got when the family attended Mass at St. Mary's Church.

Their apartment had three rooms: a kitchen; a bedroom for his parents; and a parlor where the family stayed during the day, talking, reading, visiting with friends who dropped by, and which, at night, was where both Lolek and Mundek slept.

The earthenware urn, which was majolica pottery from Italy, was filled with holy water, and Lolek had been taught to dip his fingers in it and make the sign of the cross whenever he came into the apartment or left it. There was also a prie-dieu in the parlor where his family would pray together every evening before they went to bed. On the walls of the parlor there were photographs of his family, as well as of other family members who were no longer living. From his mother's stories about them, though, Lolek felt as though they were still alive. Over the mantel there was a large portrait of his father in his lieutenant's uniform. To everyone who saw it, it was a proud reminder of the role his father had played in helping Poland win its independence from Russia.

Lolek remembered a night just a few months earlier, when his mother and father had finally decided that he was old enough to sleep in the parlor instead of in the cradle next to his mother's side of the bed. At first it had seemed strange, because he was so used to the comforting sounds of his mother's breathing; but sometimes, he admitted to himself, his father's snoring awakened him, and he didn't think he would miss that. Mundek made him feel welcome, even grown up, when he talked to him about things that had happened that day at school, as though he were another classmate instead of his little brother. It all sounded so exciting. Lolek drifted off to sleep, thinking how wonderful it would be if he could go with Mundek to school that very next day. Of course, he knew that wasn't possible, but he soon discovered that he had the next best thing. At night, before they went to sleep, Mundek would tell him what he had learned that day about the history of Poland or how to say all kinds of things in Latin. Soon, Lolek even began suggesting to his parents that everyone go to bed early so that he could learn what Mundek had learned that day.

There were so many books on the shelves that the shelves had begun to sag from their weight. After he had been sleeping with Mundek for several weeks, Lolek decided that if he couldn't go with his brother to school, he would have his own school in the parlor. During the day, when he wasn't helping his mother, while he waited for Mundek to come home, Lolek would take a book from the shelf and try to read it. Once in a while, he thought he recognized a word, so he marked that place in the book so he could ask Mundek if he was right. Often, he was, but if he wasn't, Mundek would patiently explain what the word meant. Soon, Mundek started choosing books for Lolek, telling him that these were the subjects he would be talking about that night, so it wasn't long before Lolek thought that he was doing during the day in the apartment exactly what Mundek was doing at the same time at school.

Today, Lolek had looked through a French grammar book. Mundek had already taught him how to say things in English and Latin, and tonight, he had said, he was going to teach Lolek how to say some things in French. It pleased Lolek no end that Mundek often told him that when he said the words and sentences, he sounded just like a person who lived in the country where the language was spoken. Lolek dreamed that one day he would be able to talk to people all around the world in their own languages. With Mundek's help, he decided, he could fulfill that dream.

Just then, the front door opened, and Mundek appeared, but he stopped and grinned when he saw Lolek sitting so close to the entrance.

"Have you been waiting here all day like this, Lolek?" Mundek asked.

"No, I just pulled the chair up here a few minutes ago, when I thought it was time for you to come home," Lolek replied.

Mundek dipped his fingers in the majolica urn, made the sign of the cross, and came on into the apartment. He put his book satchel on a shelf, then said, "Let me say hello to mother, Lolek, then we'll be off."

Lolek followed Mundek into the bedroom, where their mother was now propped up in bed, reading the Bible. They each hugged her.

"Do you need anything before we leave, Mother?" Mundek asked.

"No, thank you, dears. Mrs. Zamoyski should be here shortly to visit," their mother said. "When you return, Lolek, I want to hear everything you've learned about Wadowice."

"I'll tell you, Mother," Lolek promised.

As Lolek and Mundek left the apartment, they dipped their fingers in the holy water, crossed themselves, and started down the steps that led to the sidewalk.

Once outside, Mundek took Lolek's hand and said, "Wadowice is a very old town, my brother. It's been here for almost eight hundred years. There's a lot to talk about."

For the rest of the afternoon, until the sun began to set behind the Beskidys Mountains, Lolek listened as his brother told him all about their hometown.

The parish of Wadowice was made a part of

the Kingdom of Poland in 1564. In 1819, it became a part of the Austro-Hungarian Empire and home to a regiment of the emperor's troops. In 1918, after World War I, when Poland regained its independence, Polish forces took over the Austrian barracks, but it was done peacefully because the Poles in Galicia, though they considered themselves patriots, had no dislike for the ruling Hapsburgs. In fact, the people of Wadowice, along with the people of nearby Kraków, Poland's cultural center, looked more toward Vienna and Paris for inspiration than they did to Warsaw.

When Lolek and Mundek got back to the apartment, Lolek climbed the first step, then he decided to sit down on the second one.

Mundek laughed. He picked Lolek up and started carrying him up the remaining steps.

Lolek laid his head on Mundek's shoulders. "I promised Mama I would tell her everything you told me," he said. "Do you think she'll be upset if I break my promise?"

"I don't think she'll be upset at all, Lolek," Mundek said. "There'll be plenty of time to-morrow to tell her everything you saw today."

Lolek yawned. He wanted to tell Mundek how much fun he had had that day, but he was just too tired. He knew his brother would understand too.

The next morning Lolek awakened to find that Mundek had already left for school. He was disappointed. He wanted to find out what Mundek would be doing that day so he could do the same thing, but his disappointment didn't last long, as he suddenly felt as though all he wanted to do was go back to bed. As he laid his head back down on his pillow, he heard a noise coming from the kitchen and soon realized that it was his mother humming one of the hymns they often sang at church. Lolek sat up again. He couldn't remember the last time this had happened. Suddenly, he wondered if everything was all right.

He stood up and walked quietly to the door.

It wasn't fully shut, so he could see inside. His mother was standing at the cupboard, putting away some dishes, but Lolek saw that she was dressed to go out, and he wondered why.

Slowly, Lolek pushed open the door. "Mama?" he said tentatively.

His mother turned around, a smile on her face, and said, "Well, I was wondering when you'd awaken. How are you this morning?"

"Fine," Lolek replied. "I'm sorry I didn't tell you about Wadowice last night. I fell asleep."

"Oh, that's all right, Lolek," his mother said. "You can tell me later today, but now you need to get dressed because it's Thursday and we're going to the market. I want to get there before all of the best produce is gone."

Lolek grinned. He couldn't believe his luck. He had thought that it might be a while before he actually went outside again—except to the park or to Mass at St. Mary's Church—but now, the very next day, he was going to the market with his mother. He could hardly contain his excitement.

Lolek knew that market day was the most important day of the week in Wadowice. It was held just across the street, in front of St. Mary's Church. Often, Lolek had sat at a window and watched as the peasants from the countryside around Wadowice set up their stalls and sold what they had grown on their small plots of land: beetroot, potatoes, wheat.

Lolek did up his bed and dressed quickly. When his mother came out of the kitchen, he thought she looked like a picture he had seen in a magazine from Warsaw that Mr. Blamuth had given them. She had on a light yellow dress, and around her shoulders was a shawl of pale green. Her hair was piled high on top of her head, just like the women in the magazine pictures. Lolek thought his mother was absolutely beautiful.

His mother was holding two straw baskets with handles. She handed one of them to Lolek. "When we return, these will be full of God's bounty, which we'll use to nourish our bodies," she told him.

At the doorway, they dipped their fingers together in the holy water, crossed themselves in unison, and left the apartment. Even before they reached the sidewalk they could hear the noise coming from the square.

Often, Lolek knew, the sounds coming from the street bothered his mother and seemed to make her nervous, but today she smiled and said, "This is nice, isn't it?"

Lolek nodded. It was nice. It was very nice.

For the rest of the morning, Lolek and his mother strolled around the square. Lolek enjoyed watching his mother talk to the peasants, asking them about their crops, examining the potatoes, feeling them to see how firm they were, and then selecting what she thought were the best ones. Lolek could already taste them. He loved potatoes. He especially liked them boiled, then covered with butter.

From time to time his mother would encounter friends with whom she would exchange greetings, talking about one another's families. After the people left to continue their own shopping, Lolek would often hear them whisper to one another that Mrs. Wojtyla was such a charming person.

Soon Lolek's basket was full of carrots, beetroot, and cabbage, while his mother's basket was full of potatoes and onions.

After they had finally made their way around the square twice, to see if they had missed that special potato or that special onion, his mother said, "I think we need to go home, Lolek. I'm beginning to get tired."

"I can carry your basket, Mama," Lolek said.

"Oh no, dear, that's all right," his mother said. "I can manage."

But Lolek noticed that her step was not as lively as it had been earlier, and that it took them longer to get back to the apartment. When they reached the steps, his mother said, "Let's sit here for a while, Lolek, and rest."

They were still sitting there when Mundek started down the steps. "I was beginning to wonder if you had bought everything the peasants had to sell," he said brightly. He picked up both of the baskets and said, "Let's go upstairs. Father and I can prepare tonight's meal, Mama, while you and Lolek rest."

"Thank you, Mundek," their mother said.

As they started up the steps toward the apartment, Lolek said a short prayer of thanks for having had this special day with his mother. He had heard stories of how several of her brothers and sisters—and even her mother—had died too young. Those stories troubled Lolek. He only hoped that this wouldn't be the last day he spent with her.

CHAPTER THREE

THE WONDERS OF KRAKÓW

One early morning, during the late winter of 1924, Lolek was awakened by his mother's sobs. When he realized that Mundek was not lying in the bed beside him, he immediately thought that something terrible had happened to his brother, who was home for a few days from Jagiellonian University in Kraków. But as his eyes slowly adjusted to the dim light of the parlor, he saw Mundek sitting in a chair at the kitchen table.

"What's wrong?" Lolek whispered.

Mundek stood up and came back into the parlor. "It's Mama's back," he whispered. "She's in a great deal of pain, Lolek. You may have to look after yourself today."

"I can do that, Mundek," Lolek said. "I'm

four years old, and I know what to do."

Mundek lay back down beside Lolek. "I got up because I thought I might help Papa with Mama, but nothing seems to ease her pain," he said. He let out a loud sigh. "Poor Papa. He doesn't know what to do, Lolek. Neither do I."

"We can pray, Mundek," Lolek said.

"I spoke to the Virgin Mary when I awakened, Lolek," Mundek said, "but I guess it wouldn't hurt if we talked to her again."

"She'll answer our prayers," Lolek said.

Together, Lolek and Mundek got out of bed and knelt at the prie-dieu. They asked the Virgin Mary to take away their mother's suffering.

When they finished praying, Mundek looked over at Lolek and said, "My life's work will be to find a cure for whatever is making Mama suffer."

"If you don't find it, Mundek," Lolek said, "then I shall come after you and find it myself."

Mundek chuckled. "I believe you, Lolek," he said. He sighed. "I'm no longer sleepy. Let's put up the bed, and then I can make you some breakfast before I leave for Kraków."

"All right," Lolek said.

Lolek thought both Mundek and his father were good cooks. They had often taken turns preparing meals whenever their mother suffered such terrible back pains that she couldn't even walk or sew or look after Lolek. When this happened, their father closed the door to the bedroom and everyone was supposed to be very quiet.

"You're not to open the door, Lolek," his father would tell him, "unless your mother calls you."

"Yes, Father," Lolek said.

In all the times that this had happened, Lolek couldn't remember one time when his mother had called to him during the day. At first it scared him, because he was sure that something terrible had happened to her, and it was all he could do to keep from opening the door just wide enough to see if his mother was still breathing. But he willed himself to think of something else, anything else, to keep from doing it.

Usually, if Lolek sat by the window, he would let the scenes he witnessed in the street below carry him away to other places. He would pretend that he was one of the people he saw. In his head, he would follow that person, making up what happened next to whomever it was. It was strange how his mind worked, he thought, how he could go places that he had only heard Mundek or his father talk about. He often lost track of time this way, and when, in his imagination, he finally found his way back to the apartment, his father had returned. Then, for the next few hours, things would seem a little more normal.

That night, after his father had prepared the evening meal, Lolek sat by himself at the kitchen table while his father took a small tray into the bedroom and fed his mother as much as she could eat. Often it was nothing, and he returned with the food untouched, but today it was almost everything on the tray.

"Your mother must go to Kraków as soon as possible to see a physician. I'll arrange for a carriage tomorrow to take her there," his father announced to him. "You'll be going with her, and you'll be staying with your cousin Anna while the physician is looking after your mother."

Lolek found it hard to contain himself. He knew that his mother had grown up in Kraków and that there were times when she missed living in such a center of culture. He knew he himself had been to Kraków twice before, when he was just a baby, because his mother would talk to him about it sometimes, telling him how wonderful Cousin Anna had been, how comfortable she always made them feel, and how she could hardly wait to go there again, even if a visit to the doctor's was the main reason. Now, with Mundek studying at the university there, the trip for Lolek would be even more special.

Two days later, their father had arranged for a carriage and a driver to take Lolek and his mother to Kraków. After his father had stowed their small trunk in the back and tucked in the blanket around their feet, the driver cracked his whip and the carriage started through the almost-deserted streets of Wadowice.

Lolek was glad that his mother was in relatively good spirits for the trip. As the carriage left the last houses of the town behind, Lolek's mother said, "Look there, Lolek, on that hill to your right. It's the Carmelite monastery."

Lolek already knew about the history of the monastery from hearing Mundek talk about it, but he listened raptly while his mother recounted it.

Its most famous friar was Rafel Kalinowski. In 1863 he had been condemned to death for his part in the Polish uprising against the Russian czar. His life was spared, though, and he spent eight years in the frozen wastelands of Siberia. He then entered the Carmelite Order and died in the monastery almost forty years later.

Lolek's mother leaned her head back

against the carriage seat and sighed. "Oh, Lolek, the history that this road has seen," she said. She closed her eyes. "It won't be long until we pass Kalwaria Zebrzydowska," she whispered. "This is one of the holiest places in the Catholic Church, and to think it is only six miles from Wadowice."

In a voice so soft that Lolek had to put his ear almost up against his mother's mouth, she told him how the outdoor shrine had come to be.

The original owner of the land, Mikolaj Zebrzydowski, the regional governor of Kraków, built twenty-four chapels devoted to the Lenten celebration known as the Way of the Cross. It soon became the scene of a famous passion play that showed Christ's suffering and death. Years later, Zebrzydowski's son Jan built several more chapels dedicated to scenes of the life of Mary, the mother of Jesus. The faithful came from all over the Catholic world to be blessed there, sometimes traveling for days and weeks at a time.

"Your father and I will take you to Kalwaria

to be blessed, Lolek," his mother whispered, her eyes still closed. "It will change your life forever."

With that, his mother drifted off into a peaceful slumber, and for the rest of the trip to Kraków, Lolek sat in silence, not wanting to awaken his mother, whose face had never looked as peaceful as it did during the trip. It reminded him very much of the face of the Virgin Mary, which he had seen on statues in the church.

It was only when the driver stopped in front of Cousin Anna's house that Lolek gently touched his mother's shoulder and whispered, "We're here, Mama. We're in Kraków."

Before the driver could even help them out of the carriage, one of the most beautiful women Lolek had ever seen came hurrying toward them, followed by a woman wearing a black dress with a white apron and a funny white cap on the top of her head.

"Emilia! My dear Emilia!" the woman said as she reached them. "At last you're here!" She gave Lolek's mother a hug, then kissed both of her cheeks. "And this must be Lolek," she said, looking down at Lolek. "I'm your Cousin Anna, but you may not remember me." She gave him a big hug too, and Lolek thought she smelled wonderful. "The last time I saw you, you were just a tiny baby."

Lolek smiled at Cousin Anna. How wonderful it would be, he thought, to be around somebody who was this happy all the time.

Cousin Anna turned to the coachman. "Maria will show you where to put my cousins' belongings," she said to him. Lolek noticed Cousin Anna give his mother a quick glance; then, to Maria, she added, "Perhaps the rooms on the first floor would be better after all."

The driver hefted the trunk onto his shoulders as if it weighed nothing and followed Maria into the house.

Lolek looked up at the three-story building before him. The exterior was yellow plaster, with white trim all the way around. The windows had white wooden shutters.

"How many families live here, Cousin Anna?" Lolek asked.

Cousin Anna gave him a puzzled look.

"Oh, Lolek, dear, this isn't an apartment house, such as the one we live in in Wadowice," his mother said gently. "This is a house, and it all belongs to Cousin Anna."

Cousin Anna showed them to their rooms, which consisted of a parlor, a bedroom with two beds, and their own private bathroom. It was twice as large as Lolek's family's apartment in Wadowice. Lolek thought he was living in a castle.

Cousin Anna insisted that they both bathe, to relax and refresh them, and then they all sat down to a light early supper.

"Dr. Majchrowski has agreed to see you at his clinic tonight, Emilia," Cousin Anna said when everyone had finished eating. "Maria has packed a small satchel for you, with some personal items, and my driver will take you there shortly."

Lolek saw the tears start to form in his mother's eyes. "Oh, Cousin Anna, I can't thank you enough," his mother said. "I just hope the doctor can help me."

"He's the best in Kraków," Cousin Anna said. "He's better than any of the physicians in Warsaw."

When his mother was ready to leave, Lolek kissed her, then watched as she got into Cousin Anna's long black automobile and disappeared down the street.

From that moment on, the rest of Lolek's time in Kraków was almost a blur.

The next morning, after a delicious breakfast, Cousin Anna announced that the two of them were going to see all of the important sights in Kraków. With Cousin Anna driving—because she didn't want to keep giving the driver directions, she told Lolek—they headed into town.

"Kraków is the scientific, cultural, and artistic center of Poland, Lolek," Cousin Anna announced. "It was once the capital, before Warsaw, and most Poles still consider it the heart of the nation."

First, Cousin Anna showed him the royal castle and cathedral on Wawel Hill, where King John II Sobieski was buried. Next, they drove through the medieval Old Town, with its beautiful square. They passed through Kazimierz, which Cousin Anna said was the center of Kraków's Jewish religious and social life. Finally, they drove to the Jagiellonian University, with its buildings from the fourteenth century.

"Mundek is studying medicine here," Lolek announced. "He wants to find a cure for Mama's illness."

"I hope he does, Lolek. I do so hope he does," Cousin Anna said as she parked the automobile. Then she turned to Lolek and gave him a big smile. "I have a surprise for you. Once in a while, your brother will telephone me and we'll talk for a few minutes, though he's so busy, we seldom have any time to get together with each other. But today, Lolek, we're having tea with him."

Lolek gasped and clapped his hands

together. "Oh, Cousin Anna!" he said. "I was hoping this would happen!"

Cousin Anna smiled. "Now, Mundek only has a short time for us, because he's in the middle of studying for several very important examinations," she said, "so let's make the most of the few minutes we do have, all right?"

"All right," Lolek said.

At night, Cousin Anna and Lolek went to plays and operas, and Lolek was enchanted by the sights and the sounds. He was especially moved by Zygmunt Krasinski's *The Undivine Comedy*.

"It's considered the highest achievement of the Slavic theater," Cousin Anna told him.

On the last day, before Lolek and his mother were to return to Wadowice, Cousin Anna announced that she was going to take Lolek to nearby Wieliczka to see the salt mine.

"I go there often, Lolek, because to me it represents what makes the Catholic Church in Poland special," Cousin Anna said. "It always brings me peace, and it renews my spirit."

Lolek was pleasantly surprised by Cousin Anna's remarks. This was the first time that she had even mentioned the church, and he had begun to think that religion didn't play a very important role in her life.

"Mundek has only read about the salt mine, but he's never seen it," Lolek said. He grinned. "Now, when he comes home again, I'll be able to tell him all about it."

As it turned out, what Lolek saw at Wieliczka rendered him almost speechless, and he wondered if he could ever find the right words to describe this holy place to Mundek.

Salt had been dug out of the mine for almost thirty-five hundred years before the birth of Jesus Christ. At six hundred feet below the earth's surface, the deepest level of the mine, there were several chapels carved out of salt by miners. Five great salt chandeliers hung from the ceiling of the vault, and when their candles were lit, it was like standing inside a diamond that had been lit by the sun.

When Lolek and Cousin Anna returned to the surface by the steep, wooden staircase, Cousin Anna said, "Now, look around you, Lolek, and you'll see nothing but flat land. For thousands of years it has been a natural invasion route over which invaders have brought grief to us Poles, but always inside us, like the salt mine deep within the earth, has been a spirit that can never be extinguished."

Suddenly, Lolek knew that he understood exactly how his religion worked. It wasn't about what happened outside a person's body, it was all about what took place inside.

CHAPTER FOUR

SCHOOL AND THE MYSTERIES OF LIFE

Lolek's mother never talked about the week she spent at the clinic in Kraków, at least not to Lolek. Since she smiled more now, although Lolek could tell that from time to time she was in pain, he decided that whatever it was that Dr. Majchrowski did for his mother must have worked, because things in his life began to change.

That summer, Lolek and his mother began to sit in the courtyard of their apartment building, where she would visit with the other residents, or, if no one else was around, read to Lolek from books that Cousin Anna had sent back with them.

By the end of the summer, Lolek had learned the names of such Polish writers as

Adam Mickiewicz, Juliusz Slowacki, and Cyprian Kamil Norwid. Although he wasn't sure he understood everything these men wrote, he did know that one day he would read them for himself, because they were writers who his mother said would help him understand what it was like to be a Pole.

Sometimes Lolek just enjoyed sitting beside his mother, watching her sew. He knew that with Mundek at the university, the family needed more money, so his mother, who had once been a seamstress in Kraków, had returned to that trade to help make ends meet. She took in so many dresses, shawls, and women's coats for mending or repair that their apartment soon began to resemble a tailor's shop, but no one complained.

The north wind from the Baltic Sea eventually found its way to Wadowice and into the courtyard and forced them inside. Lolek's mother continued her sewing by lamplight, but Lolek's father read to him from *Quo Vadis?* by the great Polish writer Henryk Sienkiewicz.

The novel told of the introduction of Christianity to the Roman Empire while Nero was emperor.

At night, after he was in bed, Lolek often wondered what it would be like to take his religion to people who worshiped another God. Since their return from Kraków, Lolek's mother had begun to tell anyone who would listen, including his father and Mundek, when he was home, that she wanted Lolek to become a priest. When Lolek first heard her say this, he thought it was odd that she had put into words something he had been thinking about but had yet to say out loud. Would he have the strength, he wondered, to endure the punishments he knew would be inflicted on him? Would he ever deny Christ?

In September 1926, when Lolek was six, his father enrolled him in a primary school for boys that was on the second floor of Wadowice's administration building, only a few minutes' walk from the family's apartment. On the first morning of classes, Lolek kissed his mother good-bye and went out the door of their apartment and onto the street for the first time by himself. The night before, he had wondered how he would feel doing this. Would he want to turn around and go back to the security of the apartment? What he felt the moment he stepped onto the sidewalk, though, was that everything was exactly as it should be. He wasn't even sure he could explain it, but he knew that he was beginning a new and exciting period in his life.

Just as he started down the sidewalk he was hailed by two blond-headed boys heading in the same direction. They introduced themselves as Jan and Michal Polaniecki.

"I'm Karol Józef Wojtyla," Karol said. He had already decided the night before that only his family would call him Lolek. At school, he wanted to be called by his real name. "I'll be in the first grade," he added.

"Really?" Jan said. "You're as tall as I am, Wojtyla, and I'm in the third."

Karol shrugged. He had never thought about that before. Nobody had ever remarked on it.

"I'm in the first grade too," Michal said. "Are you going out for soccer? I am. I hope you will too. You'll be good, I think."

"My brother told me I should," Karol said. "So I plan to."

Jan stopped walking. "Is Edmund Wojtyla your brother?" he asked.

Karol nodded.

"He was a star soccer player when he was in school," Jan said. "If you're as good as he was, your team will never lose!"

That afternoon, their teacher, Mr. Andrzej Tyranowski, announced that for the next few days their exercise class would consist of marking off the new soccer field on land that had been donated by a wealthy Wadowice merchant.

Armed with diagrams of what a soccer field

looked like, the boys in the class headed toward a meadow that was just beyond the school.

Over the next several days, Karol and Michal, using bags of ground-up chalk, first marked the end lines and the goal lines. After that, they marked the halfway line. Mr. Tyranowski hammered a stake in the middle of the halfway line, tied a string to it, and Karol and Michal, following the circle Mr. Tyranowski made with the string, poured chalk to make the center circle. They finished by outlining the goal box and the penalty box.

The goals themselves had been donated by the same wealthy merchant who had given the school the land. They came from Vienna, the boys were told, and, Mr. Tyranowski admonished them, they had to last for a thousand years.

On the day following the completion of the soccer field, the first game was played.

"Are you ready?" Michal whispered to

Karol as they ran toward the center of the field.

"Yes, I am," Karol assured him. Although he and Mundek had kicked around a soccer ball on the streets of Wadowice from time to time, Karol had actually never played a real game before. But the night before, he had stayed up long after his parents had gone to bed reading Mundek's book of soccer rules. "Yes, I am," Karol repeated.

That day Karol scored three goals, and even though his team lost, he wasn't discouraged; but when he saw Michal's long face, he knew that his new friend was.

"Tonight, you and I shall practice our fast breaks, our feints, and our attacks," Karol said to him, pleased that he was remembering the soccer terms. "It won't be long until we're the best soccer team in our school."

Karol's prediction came true sooner than either he or Michal expected. By the end of the third week of school, they had won all but two of their daily games. By the end of the fifth week, they had won them all.

Karol's parents, seeing how much time he was spending on soccer, began to ask him questions about what else he was doing at school.

"I'm doing lots of things," Karol told them.

"Yes, but are you doing them well?" his mother asked. "If you want to be a priest, then you must know about things other than soccer."

For just a minute, Karol hesitated—not because he couldn't answer the question about life at school, but because he knew in his heart that he had begun to question whether he still wanted to be a priest. It was something he had started to pray about every night. He hadn't talked to anyone about it yet, because he didn't know himself how he really felt. He just knew that he should continue to pray about it, and that in the end God's will would be done.

"Well, Lolek?" his father said.

Lolek gave them a big smile. He opened his

satchel, took out his first report card, and handed it to his father. His mother moved closer to look on.

All of sudden, their faces lit up.

"Oh, Lolek, this is wonderful," his mother told him. She gave him a big hug and kissed him on his cheek.

"Yes, it is, Lolek," his father agreed.

He had received "very good" marks in religion, conduct, drawing, singing, and games and exercise. He had received "good" marks in language, writing, math, and science.

To help him try to understand exactly what God had in store for him when he became an adult, Karol began getting up even earlier than he needed to so he could attend Mass before school. His parents usually went in the evenings, mainly because in the morning it was now often difficult for his mother to get out of bed. Karol would still meet Jan and Michal in front of his apartment building, but when he told Michal one day what he had started doing, his friend joined him. Jan, who told them he preferred to attend Mass in the evenings, went on to school by himself. Now that it was only the two of them, Karol and Michal began to confide in each other about things that were bothering them and talked about what their teachers and Father Prochownik called the mysteries of life. Like any good detectives, they decided, they should try to solve them all.

Together, through the rest of the first grade, through all of the second grade, and most of the third grade, they tried out different answers on each other, but they were never able to come up with solutions that made sense to them.

In December 1928, when Karol was eight, he came down with the flu. He overheard his mother pleading with his father not to leave her, because she didn't want to be alone with a sick child, so his father stayed home. That day, and for several days afterward, his mother said nothing. She lay in bed, hardly moving and refusing to eat. Slowly her condition worsened, until finally, in April 1929, Karol realized that the mysteries of life would probably always remain mysteries.

CHAPTER FIVE
SAYING GOOD-BYE TO MAMA

Later, Karol would clearly remember two events of the morning of that day, April 13, 1929, that struck him as puzzling: the unusual number of blackbirds perched on a monument in the town square, and the two gypsies who crossed his path and frowned at him as he walked to school. At the time, Karol attached no particular significance to either event as a sign that this day would be unlike any other, so when his third-grade teacher and neighbor, Zofia Bernhardt, met him in the courtyard of their apartment building when he came home from a soccer game, he thought she only wanted to remind him to tell his mother that he had made a perfect score on a math quiz.

Instead, Mrs. Bernhardt, without so much as a blink of the eye, said, "Karol, your mother has died. She was taken to the hospital this afternoon. It was her kidneys and her heart. I'm so sorry, my dear child."

Karol swallowed twice, attempted to say something, but he was unable to get anything out of his throat except a gasp. For just a moment, he thought about asking Mrs. Bernhardt to repeat herself, thinking that he must have misunderstood what she had told him, but when Karol looked into her eyes, he knew he hadn't. He turned away quickly and hurried into his building.

He didn't even remember climbing up the steps, but he must have, because he was suddenly at the open front door of their apartment. It was crowded with people—more people than he ever would have thought could fit inside. They were talking quietly to his father.

When his father saw him, he stood up, blinked away some tears, and then opened his arms to receive Karol.

"Oh, Lolek, I already miss her so much," his father said. "I don't know what we'll do without her."

Karol drew back. "Does Mundek know yet?"

"Yes," his father replied. "I was able to telephone Cousin Anna in Kraków. She will get word to him and bring him here to Wadowice herself."

Three days later, a funeral Mass was celebrated for Karol's mother in St. Mary's Church. There was not room enough to hold all of the mourners who wanted to attend.

"Our mother was loved very much, Lolek," Mundek whispered to him.

Karol nodded. He was comforted by the thought that so many people in Wadowice would miss his mother too.

That night, after the last visitor had left, the three of them sat alone in the apartment in the darkness, talking softly of the things they would remember most about Emilia. Finally, they all realized that they were near exhaustion and needed to go to sleep. Before he left the room, Karol's father said, "Tomorrow, we shall make a pilgrimage to the Kalwaria Zebrzydowska shrine in honor of your mother."

A carriage draped in black cloth was waiting for them in front of the apartment the next morning. As they rode through the streets of Wadowice, the people they passed along the way gave the sign of the cross.

It was only when they had left the last houses behind that Karol remembered his mother telling him, when they were on their way to see the physician in Kraków, that she and his father would one day take him to this holy place, and indeed they had.

His mother had rallied enough from her illness on the previous August 14 that the entire family had gone to Kalwaria to celebrate the death and resurrection of the Virgin Mary. There, on the eve of the Assumption, which commemorated the departure of Mary from her earthly life and the assumption of her body into heaven, Karol and his family had joined thousands of other pilgrims accompanying the Virgin Mary to her tomb. They sang hymns and prayed as they kept watch over her all night. The next day, they celebrated her triumph over death and her entry into heaven. Karol could not have guessed at the time that his next visit to Kalwaria would be in honor of his own mother's death.

Now, as their carriage made its way to Kalwaria, Karol closed his eyes and pictured his mother instead of the Virgin Mary. In his mind, as he marched in the grand funeral cortege, it was now his mother who was laid out on the catafalque. The wooden statue, with its eyes closed in the sleep of death, carried proudly on the shoulders of men from every part of Poland dressed in their traditional costumes, had been mysteriously transformed into a statue of his mother. The Apostles, played by men whom he had often seen selling their produce in Wadowice's market square, were not weeping for Mary but for his mother. Finally, it was his mother who was taken up to heaven in the arms of God.

As their carriage left the road to make its way up to the top of Mount Calvary to the basilica built in 1658 by Bernadine monks, Karol was brought back to the present, and wondered if he, by substituting his mother for the Virgin Mary, had committed a mortal sin. He gave the sign of the cross. At his next confession, he knew, he should ask Father Prochownik for forgiveness, but instead, he decided he might just speak directly to God about why he had done such a thing.

When the carriage reached the basilica, Karol and Mundek and their father got out. Inside, they knelt at the great altar.

Each one of them prayed to the Virgin Mary to take Emilia Wojtyla, wife and mother, with her to paradise.

Karol suddenly remembered something else he wanted to do. While his father and Mundek continued to kneel at the altar, he moved quietly to a painting that was hanging over the main altar of the monastery. In the painting, the Virgin Mary's head is bowed toward the Christ Child, and the Child's nose is pressing tenderly against his Mother's cheek. Her arms enfold him.

Last year, on seeing this painting for the first time, a phrase from his Latin grammar book had suddenly come to Karol: *Totus Tuus.* It meant, "I am all yours." For days, he could not get the phrase out of his mind. It spoke to him as nothing else ever had, although he had never been sure exactly how to interpret it. Now, he believed it could apply to how he felt about his mother, his father, his brother, and certainly about God.

As Karol gazed at the painting once again, the Virgin Mary became his mother, and he became the Christ Child. Suddenly, the painting returned to its original composition, and Karol saw himself kneeling in this very spot, years from that moment. A flash of light blinded him, causing everything in the basilica to disappear, but before his eyes he saw some lines of a poem, and he whispered them.

> *On your white tomb*
> *blossom the white flowers of life.*
> *Oh how many years have already vanished*
> *without you—how many years?*
> *On your white tomb*
> *closed now for years*
> *something seems to rise:*
> *Inexplicable as death.*
> *On your white tomb,*
> *Mother, my lifeless love . . .*

Just as suddenly, the words disappeared, and try as he might, he couldn't remember them.

"Karol?"

Karol opened his eyes to see Mundek staring down at him.

"Are you all right?" Mundek asked.

Karol nodded. "Yes," he said. "Why?"

"You had the strangest look on your face,

that's why," Mundek told him. "Father's ready to leave. Are you?"

Karol nodded. He stood up, made the sign of the cross, and followed Mundek out of the basilica.

"I'm going to confession when we get back to Wadowice, Karol," Mundek told him. "Do you want to come with me?"

Karol shook his head. "No," he said.

Karol had decided that he would keep his feelings to himself after all. He only wanted to entrust to God the terrible things that happened to him in his life.

CHAPTER SIX

THE PERFECT SCHOLAR

In the spring of 1930, Karol's father borrowed an automobile from a friend to drive to Kraków for Mundek's graduation from Jagiellonian University, where he was to receive his medical degree.

As Karol and his father walked across the great Gothic courtyard of the Collegium Majus, which was founded by fourteenth-century Jagiellonian kings, Karol vividly recalled the last time he had been there. Five years earlier, he and his mother had visited Cousin Anna when his mother had come to see a physician about her back, and he and Cousin Anna had come here to have tea with Mundek. Karol wished his mother could be with the family now, in the flesh, as they celebrated this great event, but he had no doubt whatsoever that she was with them in spirit.

When Mundek's degree was conferred, his professors, dressed in their colorful academic robes, announced that he had graduated magna cum laude, with great distinction, and the audience erupted with loud applause.

After the ceremony, Mundek met them in the courtyard. "Well, I made it," he said. "I can tell you that there were times when I didn't think I would."

"What happens now?" Karol asked. "Do you come back to Wadowice?"

Mundek put his hand on Karol's shoulder. "No, Lolek, I'll be at the Children's Clinic here in Kraków for a while, then I'm going to work as a resident in a hospital in Silesia, the province where Mama's family came from."

"We're happy for you, Mundek," their father said. "You have made us all proud."

"Thank you, Papa," Mundek said. He

grinned. "I don't know about you, but I'm hungry, and Cousin Anna has prepared a graduation meal for me, so let's not keep her waiting."

As the three of them headed out of the courtyard to drive to Cousin Anna's house, Karol tried to fend off the disappointment he was feeling upon learning that Mundek would not be coming back to Wadowice to practice medicine. Ever since Mundek had gone away to school, Karol had been looking forward to the day when his brother would return, so he might regain those happy hours he had spent alone with him when he was younger, but he knew at that moment that he never would be able to relive that wonderful time in his life.

That fall, when Karol was ten, he enrolled in the Marcin Wadowita State Secondary School. It was an all-boys junior-senior high school on Mickiewicz Street in Wadowice.

In the months since his mother's death, Karol had noticed a change in his father. His life now revolved around Karol, not around his friends or his former fellow officers in the Polish army.

Each morning they rose early, prayed, and had breakfast together. When Karol became an altar boy at St. Mary's Church, they began rising an hour earlier so they could attend Mass at 7 a.m. After that, Karol would walk to school, where classes started at 8 a.m.

Often, along the way, Karol met up with Boguslaw Banas, the son of Maria Banas, who ran a bar and restaurant where Karol and his father now ate their main meal, in the early afternoon when Karol came home from school. Soon, eating at the Banases' restaurant began to feel as though Karol and his father were eating at home. Mrs. Banas had been a good friend of Karol's mother, and Mr. Banas was a friend of Karol's father. Often, Mrs. Banas would prepare special dishes for them that weren't available to the other patrons of the restaurant. Sometimes, too, Karol and his father ate at the Banases' table in their small apartment behind the restaurant.

Since Karol was allowed two hours' free time after the meal before he had to be back at his apartment to do his homework, he often stayed to play with Boguslaw. Sometimes they played with the soccer ball outside the restaurant. Sometimes they took walks through Wadowice's narrow streets. Sometimes they simply sat in Boguslaw's room and talked about whatever came to mind.

One afternoon, on one of their walks, when they passed the Wadowice Police Station, Boguslaw said, "I think I want to be a policeman, Karol."

"Really?" Karol said. "I thought you'd eventually take over the bar and restaurant when your parents can no longer run it."

Boguslaw shook his head. "Never," he said. "I want to do something more exciting than that."

"Well, Wadowice doesn't have much crime, Boguslaw," Karol said. "I don't think it would be very exciting to be a policeman here."

"Oh, I wouldn't stay here, Karol," Boguslaw

assured him. "I'd go to Kraków or to Warsaw."

"Well, Boguslaw, we need policemen to make sure we're safe," Karol said, "I think it's an honorable profession, so I hope everything works out for you."

They had now reached the front of the Banas' restaurant.

"I'll see you tomorrow, Boguslaw," Karol said. "If I don't hurry up and get back to our apartment so I can do my homework, Papa will be disappointed in me."

"You can't leave yet, Karol," Boguslaw said. "I have something to show you."

"Well, all right, but I can only stay for a minute," Karol said. "Papa is very definite about my schedule."

Together, they entered the restaurant and found it empty.

"Mama's taking a nap, before the evening customers start to come in," Boguslaw said. He grinned at Karol. "I told you I wanted to be a policeman. Well, I do, but not like Officer Havel."

Karol knew Officer Havel mostly from seeing him in the bar and restaurant, where he came to drink after duty. He also knew that Officer Havel usually went home drunk. "I don't blame you," Karol said.

"When Officer Havel thinks he's been drinking too much, he'll give his revolver to Mama before he leaves," Boguslaw said. "Mama will put it inside the cash box, and Officer Havel will come by the next morning to retrieve it before he goes to work." Boguslaw grinned. "I overheard Mama tell Papa this morning that Officer Havel was sick today." Boguslaw slowly withdrew his hand from the cash box. He was aiming a revolver at Karol. "Hands up or I'll shoot!" he said.

Karol swallowed hard. Slowly, he raised his hands. "I don't think this is . . ."

Suddenly the gun went off, and Karol felt a rush of air as the bullet flew past his head and shattered the window behind him.

Boguslaw dropped the revolver, which clattered to the floor, and covered his mouth with both of his hands.

Karol felt his stomach lurch.

Just then, Mrs. Banas appeared at the rear door that led to their apartment. "Oh! Oh!" she gasped.

Mrs. Banas spied the revolver on the floor, ran to pick it up, and put it back in the cash box. Then she turned and looked at both Karol and Boguslaw. She let out a heavy sigh. "Karol, you go on home, and Boguslaw, you go to your room," she said. "We will not speak of this."

Still shaking, Karol left the bar and restaurant without a word. By the time he got to the apartment building, he was shaking even more, so he leaned up against the exterior until he had calmed down enough to the steps to the second floor without his knees buckling on him.

Finally Karol reached the apartment, where he found his father in the kitchen, in the midst of preparing the light supper they always took together. Tonight, Karol could see, there would be bread, cheese, and fruit, but he wasn't quite sure he'd be able to eat any of it.

"I was getting worried about you, Karol," his father said. He nodded at the clock on the wall of the kitchen. "You're later than you usually are."

"Boguslaw and I walked around Wadowice, Papa. He was telling me all about how he wants to be a policeman after he finishes school," Karol said. "I'm sorry I'm late."

"Well, that's all right," his father said, "but you need to get started with your homework."

"Yes, Papa," Karol said.

Within minutes, Karol had managed to lose himself in the pages of a book about Polish history. Soon, he stopped trembling, and by that evening, after he and his father had eaten and had discussed the historical events he had read about earlier, he had almost forgotten the incident with the revolver—mainly because it was beginning to seem only like a bad dream.

Once, though, that night, he awakened in a

cold sweat, and it took him a couple of hours before he could go back to sleep. But the next morning, when he met Boguslaw to walk with him to school, nothing was said, and from that day on the memory of the event grew dimmer and dimmer.

That year, just a couple of months into school, a young priest by the name of Kazimierz Figlewicz came to Wadowice to teach catechism in the schools. Father Figlewicz was also assigned to help the altar boys who assisted the priests at St. Mary's Church during Mass.

One day, after an early Mass, Karol stopped by Father's Figlewicz's office, a small room behind the vestry.

"Hello, Karol," Father Figlewicz said, standing up and offering Karol his hand. "I'm glad it's you, because I wanted to thank you for your good work." He gave Karol a smile. "I probably shouldn't say this, but some of the altar boys aren't as conscientious as you, and I really appreciate your help."

"Thank you, Father," Karol said. He hesitated for a minute. "I want to do my best."

Father Figlewicz nodded. "You're a good role model for the other boys, Karol," he said. "You're lively, talented, sharp, and very good at everything you do. You get along well with everyone, both friends and teachers alike."

Karol blushed. He couldn't think of anything to say that wouldn't sound vain.

"I'm sorry, Karol," Father Figlewicz said. "I'm embarrassing you, and I don't mean to do that."

Karol shrugged. "It's all right," he said. Again, he hesitated. "Father, I was . . ." He stopped, unable to put into words what he wanted to say.

"Would you like for me to hear your confession, Karol?" Father Figlewicz asked.

Karol let out a heavy sigh. "Yes, Father, I would like that very much," he said. "I can talk to God about what's troubling me, but sometimes, well, even though I know I should go to confession, I just don't feel comfortable talking to all priests."

"There's nothing wrong with that, Karol," Father Figlewicz said. "It's perfectly natural, and we priests understand it."

"You do?" Karol said.

Father Figlewicz nodded. "Yes, we do," he said.

Feeling that a tremendous burden had been lifted from him, Karol confessed his sins to Father Figlewicz and, from that day forward, until Father Figlewicz was transferred to the cathedral in Kraków, he remained not only Karol's priest but his idol. Karol would often tell people that if he were ever to become a priest—which he wasn't seriously considering doing at the time—he would want to be exactly like Father Kazimierz Figlewicz.

At the end of Karol's first year of secondary school, his father received a letter from one of the teachers, which he read to Karol one evening after supper. The letter told his father that Karol stood apart from the other students. It mentioned his great composure, his talent, and his versatility. The teacher called Karol the perfect pupil, said that he was warmhearted and faithful to both his friends and his principles, and that although he was very extroverted, he was also deeply contemplative.

"She could be describing you, Papa," Karol said.

His father looked stunned. "That never entered my mind, Karol," he said.

Karol put his arms around his father and kissed him on his cheek. "You have sacrificed so much for me, Papa, and if the people at my school believe these things of me, then it is because you have taught me to be this way."

Tears formed in his father's eyes and ran down his cheeks. "You and Mundek are all I have, Lolek," he said. "God gave me and your mother great joy when he gave us you boys, and we took our responsibility for your development seriously."

On weekends, especially in the fall, Karol would hike up into the Beskidys Mountains, which surrounded Wadowice, so he could sit on a boulder or under a tree and look down on the town and think about what had happened to him that week.

Karol knew that outsiders were often surprised at how cosmopolitan Wadowice was. Though it was considered a provincial town, it didn't seem as poverty-stricken as the rest of the province of Galicia. In addition to the workers and peasants that could be found in other villages in the area, Wadowice also had artisans and intellectuals. There were three libraries, a cinema, and a theater. The state school that Karol attended was renowned for sending many of its students to Jagiellonian University in Kraków. It was only when the setting sun began to reflect off the fast-flowing waters of the Skawa River that Karol would start back down to Wadowice, filled with a calm and a peace that would last him at least through the week to come.

The following Monday at school, Karol's friend Jerzy Kluger stopped him in the hallway and said, "We looked for you after school Friday afternoon. We were going kayaking on the Skawa, remember? What happened to you?"

"I just needed to be by myself to think about something," Karol replied. "Did you have a good time?"

Jerzy nodded. "We had a great time," he said. "I only flipped over once."

"Twice," Karol said.

Jerzy blinked, then he grinned and said, "Were you hiding in the trees or something? You better not have been, or I'm going to be really angry about it."

Karol shook his head. "No. I went up into the Beskidys, but I saw some kayakers on the river. Only one of them flipped over, but he did it *twice*." He smiled. "So that was you?"

Jerzy nodded his head. "Well, they both happened so close together that it just felt like one long flip," he said. He laughed, but when Karol didn't even smile, he said, "What's wrong with you this morning?"

"Nothing," Karol said.

He started to walk away, but Jerzy grabbed his sleeve and said, "Don't tell me it's nothing, Karol. First, you don't show up for an outing we'd planned for weeks, and now, the cruelest insult of all, you don't laugh at my joke?"

"I let Gawronski copy an algebra assignment last Thursday," Karol said. "I've thought about nothing else since then, Jerzy."

Karol could tell that Jerzy wanted to explain it away by saying that everyone did that, and Karol knew that it certainly did occur from time to time, when friends either didn't understand assignments or didn't want to spend the time learning the material, but instead Jerzy said, "If it were anyone else but you, Karol, I'd think you were being silly, but—"

"But *what*?" Karol said defensively.

"Oh, please don't take offense, my friend," Jerzy said, "but you're the one person in this school who can get by with not allowing other fellows to copy his homework without a dip in popularity."

When Karol didn't reply, Jerzy added, "Look, Karol. You're the most well liked student in this school. You're everybody's idol. You're the best goalie on the best soccer team. You speak Latin. You quote Homer. You enjoy telling and listening to good jokes. You don't get into quarrels. You don't fight. You're the best friend a person can have. You don't have to explain why you don't want anybody to copy your homework."

"I want to explain it, though," Karol insisted.

Jerzy shrugged. "All right," he said. "Explain it."

"I just think it's morally wrong to deceive a teacher," Karol said. "If I let somebody copy my homework, then I'm just as guilty as the person who copied my work."

Jerzy patted Karol on the shoulder. "I'm glad to hear you say that, Karol, because frankly I think the rest of us would be very disappointed if you did it again," he said. "Like it or not, we men need at least one person in this school to be perfect so we'll have someone to pattern our lives after, and for us, that's you."

CHAPTER SEVEN

FATHER AND SON

After Karol's mother died, he and his father began spending more time together. Karol soon realized how little he really knew about his father or his father's side of the family. At night, after he had finished his homework and after they had eaten, Karol would often ask his father to talk about himself instead of the heroes of Poland.

"You're a hero to me, Papa," Karol said.

His father blushed, something Karol had never seen him do before. "You honor me with that remark, Karol," he said. "I appreciate it more than you'll ever know." He leaned back in his chair, and his eyes found the portrait on the wall that showed him and Karol's mother on their wedding day. He stared at it for a moment, then he closed his eyes.

At first, Karol thought his father had gone to sleep, for he sometimes dozed in his chair after supper, awaking in time to ask Karol if he had finished his homework before he went into the bedroom and closed the door, but this time he began to tell Karol things he had never heard before.

"Our roots are here in Galicia, Karol. The Wojtylas have always lived in this province, but for centuries we were only peasants, tied to the land. Slowly, the Wojtyla men began to learn trades, and my father became a tailor. Of course I was expected to become a tailor too, and I worked long hours in my father's shop learning how to make clothes."

"You learned well, Papa," Karol said. "I know what I wore to school today used to be an army uniform, but it doesn't look like one now."

"Yes, it's a skill that I've certainly been able to use over the years, Karol," his father said, "but I just didn't want to spend the rest of my life in our little village doing that, so I joined the army."

"Did it make you happy?" Karol asked.

His father took a deep breath and let it out before he answered. "I quickly discovered that I didn't particularly love military life for itself, Karol, but I did need the order, the discipline, and the dignity it gave me."

To Karol, what his father was telling him was a revelation. Karol had often wondered why some things—his love of order and discipline— mattered more to him than did other things, and in his father's remarks he had discovered the answer.

"I spent my entire military career first in Kraków, then in Wadowice, Karol, and so I was able to surround myself with the things that weren't available in our little village," his father continued. "Good books, music, theater, athletic events." He suddenly opened his eyes and smiled at Karol. "I also made enough money that I could ask your mother to marry me, and that is probably the most important reason why I know I made the right decision."

"Would you tell me about—" Karol started to ask, but his father interrupted him.

"Not now. I have a surprise for you." His father stood up and went to the bookshelf. "I bought two books today—used copies, both of them, but nevertheless in very good condition." He held one up for Karol to see. "It's a Polish-German Dictionary. I think you're the only eleven-year-old boy in Wadowice who is fluent in Polish, Latin, and French, Lolek, and now we're going to add German to that list."

"Oh, Papa! That's wonderful! German is the language I wanted to learn next!" Karol said. He grinned. "And what is the next book?"

His father held up the second book. "*Kritik der reinen Vernuft,*" he said. "Immanuel Kant's *Critique of Pure Reason.* It's one of the most important books ever written, Karol, and you're going to read it in the original language."

That night, together, Karol and his father translated three pages of the book. At first,

Kant's words were almost impossible for Karol to grasp, but slowly, over the next few months, as his knowledge of the German language improved, Kant's way of looking at the world began to make sense.

"I think it all comes down to this, Papa," Karol said one evening. "Kant wants to solve the conflict between the people who say that knowledge without experience is possible and the people who argue that experience is all there is. He does that by saying that our knowledge begins with experience, but it does not follow that it all arises out of experience."

His father smiled. "Karol, I think you have stated it more clearly than any professor at the university could have."

At school, if he finished his class work early, Karol would take out Kant's *Kritik* and continue reading where he and his father had left off the night before. His classmates were absolutely astounded. It seemed to them, they all said, that there was nothing Karol Wojtyla couldn't do.

"I can't imagine my father helping me translate a book from German into Polish," one classmate said.

"You're lucky to have a father who spends so much time with you, Karol," another classmate said.

When these compliments came, Karol accepted them gracefully, acknowledging that it was indeed a blessing to have a father who took such an interest in everything he did. But he also knew that there were some of his classmates who thought his father was strange.

Often, Lieutenant Wojtyla walked alone on the banks of the Skawa River, seemingly talking to himself, although Karol knew that he was in fact simply reciting some of his favorite poems. Sometimes, during the warmer months, he could also be seen swimming in the river. Once Karol had seen some of his classmates watching his father passively from the bank. Although they would never tell him, he knew what they were thinking. They were glad that Lieutenant Wojtyla wasn't their father.

Slowly, Karol came to dread holidays, especially Christmas and Easter, which for most people were family holidays. The loneliness that he and his father felt on those days was almost unbearable.

It soon became their tradition to take long walks together as a way of helping them cope with the memories that always accompanied these occasions.

But one Easter morning, after early Mass, his father said, "Today, we're going to see your Aunt Stefania, Karol. We're not going to celebrate Christ's resurrection alone."

Karol didn't want to admit that he had forgotten he even had an Aunt Stefania, but she was his father's half sister, several years older than he was, and she was not someone the family saw often. Still, on this holiday, one of the most blessed of all Christian celebrations, Karol was glad that he and his father would be with blood relatives.

With a basket of Easter eggs that Father Prochownik had blessed that morning in one hand, and with a ham in the other, Karol left their apartment with his father and, walking down a narrow road that skirted the early spring fields of wheat, they headed toward the village of Biala Leszczyny, which his father said was about an hour away.

When they arrived, they found Aunt Stefania sitting alone on the side of her bed, tears streaming down her face.

"I was praying that you'd come, Karol," she said to Lieutenant Wojtyla. "I've prayed each Easter for as long as I can remember."

"Sometimes we think we're listening to God, Stefania," Lieutenant Wojtyla said, embracing his half sister and kissing her on the cheek, "but we really aren't."

Within the hour, Karol, his father, and his aunt were seated at the small kitchen table, the Easter dinner in front of them, as they offered their prayers and asked to receive God's blessings.

At the end of the day, when he and his father were walking back to Wadowice, Karol said, "We'll no longer be alone on holidays, Papa."

His father put his arm around Karol's shoulder. "No, we won't," he said.

From then on, on most holidays, Aunt Stefania came to Wadowice to celebrate, which made Karol feel that once again, after almost two years, he now had a normal family life.

Karol could tell that the reappearance of his half sister in his life had buoyed his father's spirits too. It could still be lonely, of course, but Karol knew that the loneliness would not be unbroken.

Karol and his father still took walks, along the river and up into the mountain, and still talked to each other about the books they read, but now they also began to frequent the cinema in Wadowice, something Karol really enjoyed.

One afternoon, his father opened the newspaper, searched the bottom of the third page, and said, "What do you want to see tonight, Karol? We can go to *General Seregvo's Shame*, which is a new film, opening today, about . . . and here I'm reading what it says: 'the daughter of a Russian general who falls in love with a Polish soldier in this tragic love affair set during Russia's occupation of Poland under the czar.'"

Karol wrinkled his nose. "It sounds depressing, Papa," he said. "What's our other choice?"

"*Johnny the Musician*," his father said. "I've seen it before, and I enjoyed it very much. It's about . . . and here I'm reading again: 'a shepherd boy's journey from the country to the city, where he finds success as a musician and the love of a beautiful actress.' Originally, it was a silent movie, but the sound track was added before it reached the cinema."

"Do you mind seeing that one again, Papa?" Karol asked.

His father shook his head. "Oh, not at all, Karol," he said. "It reminds me of myself, when I went from the country to the city, so I guess it would almost, in some ways, be my story too."

Karol smiled. He had been thinking the same thing—that one day it would also be his story.

CHAPTER EIGHT

AREN'T WE ALL GOD'S CHILDREN?

By the fall of 1931, when Karol was eleven, he was beginning to find it almost impossible to shake off the melancholy feelings that now quite often simply overwhelmed him.

One afternoon, when he should have been out on the soccer field, Karol had instead taken refuge in a small room that held the school's cleaning supplies but also had a chair and a small window that let in enough light that Karol could read by it.

Earlier, Karol had borrowed a book of Shakespeare's plays in English from his former teacher, Zofia Bernhardt, but he had only gotten through the first scene of the first act of *King Lear* when he let the book fall to the floor.

Within seconds Karol was on his knees,

asking God what was wrong with him and why was he finding it harder and harder to cope with even the minor details of his life.

Suddenly, the door to the room opened and Karol saw a classmate, Jan Kus, looking at him with a puzzled expression.

"Oh, I'm sorry, Karol, I truly am," Jan stammered. "I didn't mean to interrupt your prayer."

Jan backed away, but Karol stood up and said, "It's all right, Jan. It's all right."

Jan smiled. "You're the only person I know who never gets angry about anything, Karol," he said. "I wish I knew what your secret was."

"I don't know that there's any secret, Jan," Karol said. "Maybe I'm just so confused about everything that's going on around me, I don't know when I should get angry about things."

"I don't think that's it, Karol," Jan said. "I just think you're, well, a special person, that's all."

"I should be out on the soccer field," Karol said.

"Oh, I forgot! That's why I'm here," Jan said. "Everyone was wondering why you weren't."

"Well, let's go," Karol said.

When Karol and Jan finally reached the soccer field, a cheer went up. Karol's team was down five goals to nothing when he went in, but by the time the game was over, his team had won ten goals to five. After the game, no one asked him where he had been.

No matter how much he tried to control them, Karol's moods continued to swing up and down. He knew that it bothered Jerzy Kluger to see him this way. Jerzy, who now wanted to be called Jurek, had been one of Karol's closest friends for several years, but now, this year, they had become best friends.

Jurek's father was the president of Wadowice's Jewish community and, as such, was one of the most important men in the town, but Karol knew that there were a few people in Wadowice who never mingled with Jews. He had never really understood why, although he had to admit that he felt more comfortable with Jews who wanted to assimilate into Polish society instead of those Orthodox Jews whose boys and men wore their side curls and black gaberdines.

Galicia, their province, had always been one of the major centers of Jewish culture and learning in the eastern part of Europe, and Karol and his family were well aware of how much the Jewish community contributed to the quality of life in Wadowice.

Through his friendship with Jurek—and, to a lesser extent, from having Chaim Blamuth as their landlord—Karol knew about the great festivals of Israel. He often watched the celebrations from the balcony of his apartment.

It was through Jurek that Karol met Ginka Beer, a Jewish girl. Even though Ginka's family lived in his apartment building, it never would have occurred to him to introduce himself to her.

"You should get to know her, Karol," Jurek told him one afternoon as they headed home from school. "You and she have so much in common."

From the glint in Jurek's eye, Karol knew that Jurek had more in mind than a simple friendship, but he was adamant about the fact that he would have no relationship with a girl outside of marriage, even though he knew that some of the older boys at school didn't feel the same way.

"All right, Jurek," Karol said. "I know you won't let me rest until we do this."

"You're right," Jurek said.

Almost immediately, Karol was glad Jurek had insisted on introducing him to Ginka. Within a week, he could tell that Ginka was glad to have him as a friend, because they spent hours talking about their different school subjects, debating philosophies, and discussing each other's religion. Since there were no other young people in the apartment Ginka's age, her family was more than pleased that she had Karol as a friend.

That October, on the feast of Yom Kippur, Jurek invited Karol and his father to temple to hear Moishe Savitski, a new recruit at the infantry regiment in Wadowice, sing the Kol Nidre.

"May I invite Ginka to come with me?" Karol asked Jurik.

"Of course," Jurik said. "I expected you to do that."

That evening Karol listened intently, stirred by Savitski's voice and awed by the chants in which Israel confessed its sins and entrusted itself to God. From time to time, Karol would steal a glance at Ginka. Mostly she kept her eyes on Savitski, but occasionally she would turn her head just as Karol was about to look away and give him a friendly smile. It was during those moments that Karol remembered that the last woman who had smiled at him that way was his mother.

★　★　★　★

The next day, after school, Jurek said, "Well, Karol, what did you think about the service last night?"

"I think that if I weren't Catholic, Jurek, I'd be Jewish," Karol replied.

"That's a very diplomatic answer," Jurek teased him. "I think that's why my grandmother likes you so much."

"When did she tell you that?" Karol said.

"*When?*" Jurek said. "Why, every time I visit her, that's when."

Karol laughed. "I'm sorry, Jurek," he said. "Just for your sake, I'll make sure I'm unpleasant to her the next time I see her."

"You'll have your chance in a few minutes," Jurek said, "because she told me to invite you to our house today so she can have tea with us."

"Really?" Karol said. "She actually wants to have tea with me this afternoon?"

"Oh, don't act as if you aren't aware of how my family feels about you, Karol," Jurek said with mock anger. "They hold you up to me all the time as an example of how a good Jewish boy should behave."

Karol stopped walking and bent over laughing. "Imagine that, Jurek," he managed to say between gasps for breath.

The tea was delicious and so was the cake, which Jurek's grandmother said that she had herself baked especially for Karol. When she offered Karol a second piece, he declined politely, causing Jurek's grandmother to turn to Jurek and say, "Karol is so well mannered, such a good student, so hardworking. Couldn't you be a little bit more like him?"

Jurek rolled his eyes at Karol. "See what I have to put up with every day of my life because of you?" he said.

It snowed heavily on New Year's Eve, 1931, keeping most of Wadowice inside to celebrate, but Ginka had invited Karol and Jurek to her family's apartment to ring in the New Year, and they both arrived at the same time, although Karol could tell that Jurek was upset about something.

When Ginka opened the door, she said, "Where's Pola, Jurek?"

Jurek frowned. "She decided not to come with me," he said.

Karol gave Jurek a puzzled look. "Who's Pola?" he asked.

When Jurek didn't answer him, Ginka said, "Pola Boniecki, the niece of the man who owns the cinema here in Wadowice. She's visiting from Kraków. Jurek and I met her last night after the movie. I invited her to celebrate New Year's with us, and Jurek said he'd come by for her."

"I don't want to talk about it," Jurek said.

"So when you arrived at Mr. Boniecki's house, Pola said that you should have told her you were Jewish, because she doesn't go out with Jewish boys, didn't she, Jurek?" Ginka continued.

"Yes!" Jurek said through clenched teeth.

"Ginka?" Mrs. Beer called. "Why don't you invite your guests inside?"

For the next two hours, Ginka did everything she could to lift Jurek's spirits by telling jokes, by showing them different card games, and by playing charades, but nothing worked. When the Beers' large mantel clock finally struck midnight and everyone toasted the New Year, Karol couldn't remember ever having spent a longer two hours.

As they said their good-byes at the door, Jurek apologized for ruining the party, but Ginka said, "I just enjoyed your being here, both of you, but I'm sorry, Jurek, that you've had to experience this so soon."

Together, Karol and Jurek walked across the courtyard to the Wojtylas' building, but just as Karol was about to go inside, Jurek tugged on his sleeve and said, "Not yet, please, Karol. I'm not ready to be alone."

Turning up the collars of their coats and pulling their caps down over their ears, they started through the deserted streets of

Wadowice, not saying anything to each other until they were two blocks beyond the town square.

"From time to time, I hear my parents talking about what it means to be a Jew in Poland, Karol," Jurek said, "but until now, it has just been talk."

"That's all it ever will be, Jurek," Karol said. "Talk."

"Are you sure?" Jurek asked.

Karol thought for several minutes before he finally answered. "No, I'm not sure," he said. "I guess I was only hoping it would be."

"I remember what you told that woman in your church, when I came by once to get you because you were supposed to be at a soccer game," Jurek said. "I'll never forget it, in fact."

Karol nodded. "I meant it," he said.

"'Why is the son of the president of the Jewish community standing next to the altar of our church?'" Jurek said in a woman's voice.

"'Aren't we all God's children, my good woman?'" Karol said, repeating his part.

Together, they laughed at the memory, but then Jurek said, "I could see it in her eyes, Karol. Her answer, if she had given one to you, would have been, 'No!'"

CHAPTER NINE
GOD'S WILL

In March 1932 Karol arrived home from school one day to find his father reading a letter with tears streaming down his face.

"Papa!" Karol cried. "What's happened?"

His father looked up, but instead of the grief that Karol had expected to see on his father's face, he saw joy instead, and now Karol was even more puzzled than ever.

"It's a letter from Mundek," his father said. "He's in Bielsko, at the hospital there, and he says that visits home will be easier now."

Karol started jumping up and down. Suddenly, his father grabbed hold of Karol's hands and started jumping up and down with him.

"Mundek's coming home!" they sang together. "Mundek's coming home."

All of a sudden Karol's father stopped and stared at the front door to the apartment. He had a huge grin on his face.

Karol turned. Jurek was standing there watching them with wide open eyes.

"Come in, Jurek, and join us," Lieutenant Wojtyla said. "We've just received some good news. Mundek will soon be able to visit us more."

Jurek came on inside, joined the circle, and soon the three of them were dancing all over the parlor.

When they finally stopped, exhausted, Jurek said, "I can't imagine my father ever doing anything like this, Lieutenant Wojtyla, but that's why I like coming over here so much."

Mundek was true to his word. Two weeks later, he showed up, driving a car he had borrowed from another one of the residents. For Karol, these visits were a return to the happier days he remembered so fondly.

On some visits, Mundek showed Karol and his friends the finer points of soccer—not only on the field, but also in the streets of Wadowice, where they could often be seen dribbling the balls.

Mundek was also a champion bridge and chess player. Within weeks after he taught Karol and Jurek how to play both games, his championship was challenged.

That summer, Karol and Mundek took long hikes in the Beskidys Mountains and swam in the Skawa River.

In September, after an early and very heavy snowfall, Mundek taught Karol how to ski.

"I may not be home as much for several weeks," Mundek told Karol and their father as he finished packing his belongings to return to Bielsko at the end of one visit. "This is always a bad time of the year for epidemics of one kind or another, and we're already understaffed at the hospital."

"You'll be home for Christmas, won't you?"

Karol said. "It wouldn't be the same if you weren't."

"Of course I'll be home for Christmas, Lolek," Mundek. "I wouldn't miss that for the world."

All during October and November, Karol thought of almost nothing else, but instead of this affecting his studies, it seemed to increase his academic abilities, which few of his friends or teachers thought was possible.

On the morning of December 1, Karol met Jurek outside their apartment and said, "It won't be long now!"

"I'm looking forward to Mundek's coming home for Christmas almost as much as you are, Karol," Jurek said. "I've figured out several new chess moves I want to show him."

December 1, 1932, was cold and blustery, but Karol, on the way home from school, saw that as a positive sign. It had not snowed very much since September, and he had been hoping that the weather would change so that by the time

Mundek came home for Christmas, the snow-pack on the mountains would be perfect for skiing.

When he opened the door of their apartment, though, he knew immediately that it really didn't matter if it ever snowed again. Once he saw his father's pained expression and eyes swollen from crying, he knew it could only be one thing.

"Mundek is dying, Karol," his father managed to say between sobs. "We have to leave for Bielsko at once."

When Karol and his father arrived, they went immediately to the hospital. The senior physician, Dr. Brücken, met them at the entrance.

"Please come this way," Dr. Brücken told them somberly.

Karol and his father followed the doctor to a room where they thought they would find Mundek, but instead it turned out to be Dr. Brücken's office.

"Why are we here, Dr. Brücken?" Lieutenant

Wojtyla demanded. "We should be with Mundek. He needs us."

"I have to see my brother," Karol managed to say.

Dr. Brücken shook his head. "I'm afraid that's impossible," he told them. "He's in quarantine, and we can't allow you inside."

Karol could feel the anger surging up inside him, making him want to scream, but he managed to control it long enough so that he could ask Dr. Brücken to tell them exactly what had happened.

"Of course," Dr. Brücken said. He picked up a telephone on his desk, said something so faint that Karol couldn't understand it, then hung up the receiver. "I've asked to have tea brought to us," he said.

"Thank you," Karol managed to say.

"In late November, a young girl was admitted to our hospital," Dr. Brücken began. "She had scarlet fever, which, as you may know, is a very infectious disease."

Karol had heard of the disease, but he didn't

know much more about it than its name.

"It's usually fatal because there's no treatment for it," Dr. Brücken continued, "and about all we can do is put the patients in an isolated wing of the hospital and leave their care to volunteers of local charities."

"That sounds barbaric," Lieutenant Wojtyla said quietly.

Karol looked at his father. He had never heard him express such anger before.

"I agree, sir, but it's important to realize that the disease can be spread by healthy people as well as those who have been infected by it," Dr. Brücken said. "If our medical staff treated the patients with scarlet fever, while we might not be infected ourselves, we could certainly infect our other patients, especially those in weakened conditions."

"I'm sorry. I shouldn't have said that," Lieutenant Wojtyla said. "I shouldn't have said that."

"But how did Mundek get the disease?" Karol asked.

Dr. Brücken looked directly at Karol. "He felt the same way your father does," he replied. "He thought it was unjust to leave sick people to themselves only because of the fear of contagion, so he offered to help the girl."

"I'm proud of him for doing that," Lieutenant Wojtyla said.

"He knew the danger he faced, and he knew that he had no obligation to the girl, because she wasn't even his patient," Dr. Brücken said, "but he said it was his duty as a doctor and as a Christian to make sure that someone who was ill was not simply abandoned."

For three days, Karol and his father stayed at the hospital, sometimes weeping and inconsolable because they were unable to give any comfort to Mundek.

"I want to kiss him, Karol," his father sobbed. "I want to caress him as I did when he was just a child, and tell him that I love him."

Karol nodded. "I don't want Mundek to die alone, Papa," he said.

Finally, on the evening of December 4,

Mundek died. The hospital, wanting to honor Mundek's charitable service, posted the announcement not only inside the hospital but all around Bielsko. According to Renzo Allegri's biography, *John Paul II: A Life of Grace*, the announcement read:

> *Dr. Edmund Wojtyla, age twenty-six, assistant at the Community Hospital in Bielsko, came to rest in the arms of Our Lord at 7:00 p.m. on December 4, 1932, after receiving Extreme Unction and offering his young life for suffering humanity. Greatly saddened by the loss of our dear colleague and beloved coworker, let us pray to the Almighty that his soul may rest in peace.*

The announcement and the reports in the newspaper so moved the people of Bielsko that a large crowd attended Mundek's funeral on December 6.

At the cemetery, Karol, standing alongside

his father, listened to the words of Dr. Brücken's eulogy, which told of his brother's last tortured moments on earth. But as Karol fingered his brother's stethoscope around his neck, which had been presented as a gift to him by the hospital staff the previous day, he tried only to remember the many happy hours he had shared with his brother instead.

As Karol and his father left the cemetery, having said their good-byes to Mundek, Karol found that he was suddenly remembering, with a clarity he had never known before, the apocalyptic accounts in the Bible of death, judgment, heaven, and hell.

It was close to evening when Karol and his father arrived back in Wadowice. Lieutenant Wojtyla went straight to the apartment without a word, but Karol knew that he couldn't at that moment face the rooms where he had spent so many happy hours with his brother. Instead, he decided to go into the courtyard, but he only got as far as the gate.

Later—Karol couldn't be sure how long it

had been—their neighbor, Helena Szczepanski, who sometimes cleaned their apartment for them, found him there.

She took Karol in her arms, hugged him tightly, and said, "Poor Lolek, you've lost your brother."

Mrs. Szczepanski's remark seemed to break the spell he was in. Karol looked up at her, studied her face for a moment, then said, "It was God's will."

With that, he turned and headed toward his apartment. From that day forward, Karol decided, he would lock himself up in silence.

CHAPTER TEN

LIFE IS A STAGE

After Mundek's death, Karol once again felt hollow inside. For his father's sake, though, he re-created a social, self-confident outside, and he began to realize that it was like playing a part in a play. When he was around other people, he was performing, but once he was by himself, off stage, he retreated into his books more than ever to help him deal with the tortures of his life.

Karol was especially fascinated by the language and the literature of Poland. Remembering how he had once delighted in his father's reading of Sienkiewicz's *Quo Vadis?*, he now devoured the novel for himself, and when he finished that, he also read Sienkiewicz's *With Fire and Sword* and *The Deluge*. Within weeks, he was able to recite long passages by heart from all three books.

It was poetry, though, which Karol loved most of all, and his favorite poet was Adam Mickiewicz, who had been a champion of Polish independence. At times, Karol thought about trying to become the next Mickiewicz, and he spent long hours writing and polishing his poetry. He was never unhappy with what he wrote, although he never felt that his words carried the authority of Mickiewicz's works.

When Karol was fourteen, in 1934, he discovered the theater. Later, after he had thought about it, wondering why this interest had struck him like a thunderbolt, Karol believed that it was Mickiewicz's cadenced language, which Karol would recite out loud when he was by himself, that turned him in that direction.

When Karol mentioned his interest to one of his classmates, Antoni Bhodanowicz, Antoni said, "That makes sense, Karol. You're starting to look like a leading man."

The comment somewhat embarrassed Karol. He had never thought of himself as anyone's love interest, although he knew that he had slimmed down in the last couple of years and that his participation in sports had given him an athletic build, which some of the girls noticed. He had also overheard several of them talking about his beautiful blue eyes. For his part, though, Karol was more interested in the theater as a means to present powerful messages to the audience who attended the plays than he was in using it as a showcase for his physical self.

All of his teachers immediately noticed the change in Karol, and because he was so well liked and because everyone wanted to do something to help bring him out of what they all recognized as a melancholy brought on by personal tragedies, they began to encourage this interest in theater by giving him copies of their favorite plays. Karol read them all, several times, each time playing a different role.

One afternoon, the stationmaster's son, Zbigniew Silkowski, hurried up to him and breathlessly said, "My sister thought I had invited you, and I thought she had invited you, so it was only just now that we realized that you hadn't been invited."

Karol grinned at him. "Zbigniew, you're not making any sense," he said. "What are you talking about?"

"Some of us are getting together at my house after school for dramatic readings, Karol," Zbigniew said. "We want you to come. Will you?"

"Oh, of course," Karol said. "I'd like to very much."

That afternoon, Karol hurried home, dropped his satchel on the kitchen table, spent a few minutes looking through his books to find just the right passages for the reading, then finally settled on a book of poems by Mickiewicz and headed for the stationmaster's house.

Karol was the last one to arrive, but when

he appeared at the door of the parlor, everyone stopped talking and Zbigniew said, "We thought you might have forgotten."

"Oh no, never," Karol said.

That afternoon, Karol mesmerized everyone as he spoke Mickiewicz's powerful words. When he tried to sit down, the rest of the students wouldn't let him. They insisted that he keep reading, and when he had gone through all of Mickiewicz's poems once, they insisted that he start all over.

Finally, Mrs. Silkowski had to intervene, saying that although it would have been her pleasure to invite everyone to supper that night, she hadn't counted on their being there that late, so she hadn't cooked enough food.

As Karol made his way back to the apartment, he was accompanied by three of his classmates who insisted that he recite more of Mickiewicz's poetry.

When they reached the gate of Karol's building's courtyard, the students wouldn't let him leave until he had finished the poem he had started. By the time he got up to his apartment, he could hardly talk, he was so hoarse, but it had been a long time since he had felt so happy.

The next morning Karol's throat was still a little raw, but his father suggested he gargle with salt water, which he did, and by the time he got to school that morning, his voice had returned.

Several of the students who had attended the dramatic readings the afternoon before stopped him and told him how much they had enjoyed it.

As Karol was about to go into his Latin classroom, he was stopped by Mr. Mieczyslaw Kotlarczyk, the man who taught Polish literature at his school.

"We're forming a troupe of young actors from both the boys' and girls' high schools, Karol," Mr. Kotlarczyk told him. "Our first meeting is today after school, in my classroom, and we want you to join us."

"I'll be there," Karol said.

★ ★ ★ ★

When Karol got to Mr. Kotlarczyk's classroom that afternoon, he was delighted to see Ginka Beer in the group.

"I want to introduce you to someone," Ginka said, taking him by the hand and pulling him toward the back of the room.

The crowd of students in the room parted for them, revealing one of the most beautiful girls Karol had ever seen.

"Halina, this is—," Ginka started to say, but Halina interrupted her with, "Oh, you don't have to tell me who this is, Ginka. I'd know those blue eyes and that thick, blond hair anywhere." She gave Karol a sparkling smile and offered him her hand. "Halina Królikiewicz," she said. "If you recognize my last name, it's because my father is the director of your school."

"I'm very happy to meet you," Karol said. He tried to keep his voice steady, but he didn't think he had been very successful. "I'm really looking forward to being a part of this theater group."

For the group's first performance, which was staged in Wadowice's park, Mr. Kotlarczyk chose a mixture of romantic poetry and popular songs, which he knew would especially showcase the talents of Karol and Halina. He was right. They became instant stars.

They also became instant friends and were soon almost inseparable. For Karol, the attraction was more of a competitive nature instead of a physical nature, but it was obvious to everyone how much they liked each other. In the Poland of that time, though, for two teenagers brought up in a rigid Catholicism, the relationship would remain restrained and pure.

"You're a natural, Karol," Mr. Kotlarczyk told him one day. "I'm not only naming you the group's director but the set designer as well."

"I'm honored, sir," Karol said. "I'll do my best."

"Of course, you'll probably be starring in most of the productions too, Karol," Mr. Kotlarczyk added, "so we may just rename this the Karol Wojtyla Theater Group."

Karol grinned. "Halina might have something to say about that," he said.

Someone punched his shoulder playfully. He turned to see Halina smiling at him.

"You're right about that," Halina said.

That week the group went into rehearsals for Juliusz Slowacki's *Balladyna*. Karol was assigned the role of Kirkor, the main character, but two days before the opening night, the student assigned to play the role of Kostryn dropped out.

"This is terrible," Mr. Kotlarczyk said to the hastily assembled cast. "We may just have to cancel the show."

"We don't have to do that. I can play both parts," Karol told them. "Kostryn doesn't appear until after Kirkor has died."

Karol was true to his word. He played both roles magnificently.

"How did you ever learn the part of Kostryn in such a short time, Karol?" Ginka asked him after the play was over.

Karol smiled. "I had already learned it during rehearsals," he told her.

As a director, Karol often chose plays with patriotic themes, and the group was soon in great demand around Wadowice. It wasn't long, though, before word of their troupe spread beyond Wadowice, and they took their performances on a tour of some neighboring villages and the Kalwaria Zebrzydowska shrine.

Although Karol's choice of plays varied, the cast never did. He almost always had the leading roll. In Wyspianski's *Sigismund Augustus*, he was the king. In Sophocles's *Antigone*, he took the role of Haemon. With Mr. Kotlarczyk's help, Karol adapted the book of Revelation, and he played the part of John the Baptist. Halina was always his leading lady.

One spring afternoon, just before the troupe was to have a meeting to decide on its next performance, Halina pulled Karol aside and said, "I've just learned that Kazimiera Rychterówna is coming to Wadowice in two weeks, Karol. I can hardly believe it."

Karol could hardly believe it either. Kazimiera Rychterówna was the most famous actress in Poland. "Do you think we could get her to judge a recitation contest between the two of us?" he asked mischievously.

Halina raised an eyebrow and said, "I think we can. I'll talk to my father about it."

Two days later, Karol and Halina were informed that Miss Rychterówna had indeed agreed to judge the contest, so they immediately began to prepare for their performance.

Karol chose *Promethidion*, by Norwid, whom he admired because the poet's style was obscure and his sentences often difficult to understand. The night of the performance, as Karol had hoped, he was able to recite Norwid in such a way that people in the audience who thought they would never understand the poet were swept away by Karol's strong tone and his ability to get to the heart of the meaning of the text. Karol didn't win, but he made a deep impression on those in attendance.

The next day, after both Karol and Halina had received hearty congratulations from Mr. Kotlarczyk and the members of their acting troupe, Karol whispered to Halina that he wished he had chosen another one of Norwid's poems.

"Are you saying that with a different poem you could have beaten me, Karol?" Halina teased him.

"Oh no, not at all, Halina. You gave an absolutely brilliant reading," Karol assured her, "but if I had chosen Norwid's *Polish Jews*, then I could have reminded everyone in the audience of what happened to the Jews in Warsaw in the 1860s, when the Cossacks broke up an anti-Russian demonstration."

Halina gave him a puzzled look. "Why would anyone want to be reminded of that, Karol?" she asked.

"Because Norwid talks about Poland's priceless heritage of two great cultures, Halina," Karol said. "Polish and Jewish." When Halina didn't say anything, Karol added, "With all the terrible things that are happening now to the Jews in Germany, I just think we Poles need to remember that."

CHAPTER ELEVEN

GRADUATION DAY

In 1935, when Karol was fifteen, he became president of the Marian sodality, an organization dedicated to veneration of the Virgin Mary. Karol did such a good job, he was re-elected president for a second year.

Karol was also chosen to head the Abstinence Society in Wadowice. The members of this group made it their mission to keep young people from drinking alcohol and smoking cigarettes. While very serious about abstinence, Karol was not fanatical, and he understood that human beings weren't perfect and that occasionally some of his classmates would surrender to temptation. In fact, one cold winter day, when he and a group of friends were returning by an unheated train to

Wadowice from an outing near Warsaw, he took a sip of brandy from a bottle that was being passed around.

When someone later asked him why, he said, "I was freezing, that's why, and it started my blood circulating again. It isn't called 'eau-de-vie' in French for nothing."

Because Karol was such a good soccer player, he often played on a lot of different teams in Wadowice. One Sunday in 1936, the day after Karol had scored the winning goal of the Jewish soccer team, Father Prochownik read a letter at Mass that had been sent to every parish by the Cardinal Augustyn Hlond, the Catholic primate of Poland. According to *His Holiness: John Paul II and the History of Our Time* by Carl Bernstein and Marco Politi, the letter read:

> *"There will be a Jewish problem as long as the Jews remain. It is a fact that the Jews are fighting against the Catholic*

Church, persisting in free thinking, and are the vanguard of godlessness, Bolshevism, and subversion. It is a fact that the Jews deceive, levy interest, and are procurers of immorality. It is a fact that the religious and ethical influence of the Jewish young people on the Polish people is a negative one."

Without further comment, Father Prochownik laid the letter on the pulpit and began a final prayer.

Instead of bowing his head, Karol looked over at his father, whose eyes were still open and staring straight ahead.

Later, at home, Karol said, "How could Cardinal Hlond say something like that? We don't feel that way, Papa. Jurek and Ginka are my friends. Just because they don't believe as we believe doesn't mean they're evil."

For several minutes his father remained silent, his chin resting on his chest, but then, finally, he looked up at Karol and said,

"Wadowice is unusual, Karol, because up until now, anti-Semitism hasn't been a problem. But in the rest of Poland, it's ingrained and widespread, and what is happening now in Germany is only making it worse."

Karol knew all about what the Nazis were doing in Germany. Sometimes Ginka and Jurek talked about it, but Karol always reassured them that that would never happen to them in Wadowice. Now, he wasn't so sure.

For a while, Wadowice really did seem safe for everyone. But then, in the spring of 1937, a few young hoodlums began smashing windows of some of the Jewish shops. Most people thought it was more a criminal act than anything against the Jews, and for the next few weeks, they seemed to be proven correct because nothing else happened.

At the beginning of summer, though, Ginka appeared unexpectedly at the front door of Karol's apartment.

"Well, this is a surprise," Karol said. Although he and Ginka were extremely close, and although he had been to her family's apartment, she had never come to his because her family thought it would be improper. "Come in!"

"How are you today, Ginka?" Lieutenant Wojtyla asked.

Ginka opened her mouth to reply, but she suddenly burst into tears instead, and Karol led her to a chair so she could sit down.

"My father has resigned as manager of the bank, and we're emigrating to Palestine," Ginka sobbed. "He thinks Poland is no longer safe for Jews."

Karol was so stunned and upset by Ginka's news that he couldn't speak.

"Not all Poles are anti-Semitic, Ginka!" Lieutenant Wojtyla said. "You know we're not!"

"I know, sir, but not all Poles are like you and Karol," Ginka to him. "There are a lot of people in Wadowice who are demanding that people boycott Jewish shops and businesses, and if that happens, my family will have no

135

way to make a living." Ginka turned back to Karol. "Won't you please say *something*?"

Karol still could find no words, but he felt his face turning red from uncontrollable anger. He could only think that once again he was going to lose someone he loved.

Finally, Ginka said, "Karol, I shall never forget you, truly, and I promise that I'll write you once we reach Palistine. Know that. Even if my letters never reach you, they were written and sent."

When Karol still said nothing, Ginka shook hands with Lieutenant Wojtyla and left.

As soon as the door was closed, Karol burst into tears. His father embraced him, and together the two of them cried on each other's shoulders.

Later that night, Karol went to the Beers' apartment, where he found the family frantically packing their belongings. He tried to persuade Ginka to stay, saying that he and his father would give her the bedroom in their apartment until they could find more suitable quarters for her, but Ginka kissed him lightly on the cheek and whispered, "One day, Karol, after this terrible time is over, we'll meet again."

Karol sadly said good-bye to the Beer family. Outside, in the courtyard, he leaned up against a wall, wondering how many more times his heart could be broken before it would refuse to heal again.

Now Karol began to spend more time in church, in silent meditation, but instead of his parish church, he chose the convent church of the Carmelite Order. He would sit for endless hours praying in front of the Virgin Mary.

Soon, Karol began to talk to one of the priests, Father Józef Prus, who was also the rector of the Carmelite High School and who knew Karol from his theatrical performances in Wadowice. Father Prus had always assumed that Karol would become an actor after graduation, but Karol confided to Prus that he was in search of spiritual guidance in his life.

Father Prus gave Karol his first book on Saint John of the Cross. Karol found himself strongly attracted to the ways of the Discalced Carmelite monks who spent their days in silence, concentration on God, and penance. At a time when the rest of his classmates were turning more toward secular behavior, Karol's commitment to the Christian life became even more rigorous.

Every first Friday of the month, as was his practice since entering high school, Karol went to confession and took communion, but where once this had just been part of a routine, it now began to take on more meaning. Karol wasn't sure he understood exactly what was happening to him, but he did know that, through prayer, he could deal with the pain of his human suffering.

On May 6, 1938, the archbishop of Kraków, Adam Stefan Sapieha, arrived in Wadowice to administer the sacrament of confirmation to

Karol's high school class before they graduated. In doing this, the church gave the Holy Ghost to those who had already been baptized, in order to make them strong and perfect Christians and soldiers of Jesus Christ.

Karol was given the honor of welcoming Archbishop Sapieha in the name of the students. He greeted the Archbishop in perfect Latin.

Archbishop Sapieha looked at Karol for several seconds, then he turned to Father Edward Zacher, Karol's religion teacher.

"What will this young man do after graduation?" he asked. "Will he enter the seminary?"

"Sir, may I have permission to answer that?" Karol said.

Somewhat taken aback, Father Zacher said, "Yes, Karol, you may."

"I'm going to Jagiellonian University to study literature and philosophy," Karol said.

"What a pity," Archbishop Sapieha said. He turned to Father Zacher. "I think this young man could go far in the church, and I have the feeling, Father Zacher, that I have not seen the last of him."

On May 27, 1938, Karol graduated from high school. He was the class valedictorian.

That night, at the commencement ball, the new graduates danced far into the night.

Karol thoroughly enjoyed dancing, especially with Halina, but their relationship on the dance floor was always formal.

After each dance, whether it was a polonaise, a mazurka, a waltz, or a tango, all of the boys, Karol included, would escort their partners back to their chairs, seat them, and then give a deep bow.

Over the next few days, Karol and the rest of the graduates said their good-byes to one another, but his parting from Jurek had a sense of foreboding about it, because conditions for the Jews of Poland were worsening.

"I shall pray for you and your family daily, Jurek," Karol told him.

"Thank you, Karol," Jurek said. He turned

to leave, then stopped and added, "Don't forget, will you?"

"I won't forget," Karol assured him.

One week later, Karol began his required national service on a road construction job in the town of Zubrzyca Górna. He had been looking forward to the outdoor physical activity, but for the next month he ended up mostly peeling potatoes.

In August, Karol and his father left for Kraków, where Karol would begin his studies at Jagiellonian University in the fall. As Karol watched Wadowice recede from view, he had the strangest sensation that had just awakened from a dream.

CHAPTER TWELVE
WORLD WAR II

When the Wojtylas first arrived in Kraków, Lieutenant Wojtyla told Karol that, before he died, he wanted his son to promise that he would commit himself to God's service as a priest. But Karol could only promise his father that he would pray about the matter day and night. For the time being, he said, he would continue with his plans to enroll at Jagiellonian University to study literature and philosophy. Since Karol was still very interested in a career in the theater, he also joined an experimental theater group. Just as he had in Wadowice, he participated in poetry readings and literary discussion groups too. Those who knew him said that he was a very gifted actor and a fine singer.

In 1939, after the Germans invaded Poland, Jagiellonian University was closed. When the Germans started rounding up all out-of-work Polish men so they could be sent to camps in Germany, Karol escaped deportation by taking a job in a quarry in Zakrozowek, near Kraków, that supplied the occupation forces with building stones.

In February 1941, Karol came home from the quarry to find his sixty-one-year-old father dead. Now, he was all alone.

Over the next few months, Karol pushed himself harder than he ever had before, trying to numb the pain of his personal grief, but nothing he did seemed to work. To this was also added the helplessness he felt because he couldn't do anything to rid his beloved Poland of the hated Nazis. Through all of this, though, Karol still continued to pray for spiritual guidance in his life.

In early 1942, Karol was transferred to the Solvay Chemical Works, which, as it turned out, made it easy for him to continue his studies at the reopened Jagiellonian University.

In October of that same year, believing now that what his parents had wanted for him was also what God wanted for him, Karol entered the School of Theology with the intention of becoming a priest; for an emotional outlet, he also continued to act in plays.

In August 1944, the Polish Home Army rose up against the Germans in Warsaw, taking the Nazis by surprise. Hitler ordered his troops to crush all resistance. Since the Germans were sure there would also be an uprising in Kraków, they began rounding up all the men, house by house. Karol was in his little basement apartment on Tyniecka Street when he heard shouts and the pounding footsteps of the German soldiers. He got down on his knees and started to pray. Overhead, he could hear the soldiers as they charged up and down the stairs, but for some reason they never found the door leading to Karol's basement apartment. After that, Karol stopped attending classes at the university and going to his job at the chemical works, completely dropping out of sight of the Nazi occupiers.

Archbishop Sapieha had moved his seminarian students into his residence to finish their training in an "underground" seminary he conducted there. Karol decided to take refuge in the archbishop's residence so he could continue his studies for the priesthood. He remained there until Soviet forces liberated Kraków from the Germans on January 18, 1945.

Karol's journey toward the priesthood included all the stages called for by the church before the Second Vatican Council. In September 1944 he was tonsured in a ceremony in which a circlet of hair was cut off the crown of his head to show that he was now a cleric. The following December, he received the first two of what are called the minor orders, that of porter and lector.

In December 1945, he received the two other minor orders, that of exorcist and acolyte.

Finally, in 1946, Karol completed his studies and the reception of orders, with Subdiaconante on October 13, Diaconate on October 20, and Priesthood on November 1, the Solemnity of All Saints. Karol's priestly ordination was performed by Cardinal Adam Sapieha in his private chapel.

The next day, November 2, 1946, Karol celebrated his first Mass in the crypt of Saint Leonard, located in Wawel Cathedral, Kraków, Poland's national sanctuary.

CHAPTER THIRTEEN

THE PRIESTHOOD YEARS

Karol served as a chaplain to university students at St. Florian's Church in Kraków during the early years of his priesthood. Since the church was located next to Jagiellonian University, it was convenient for him to continue his work on a second doctorate in philosophy.

In 1954, when Poland's Communist government abolished the university's theology department, the entire faculty moved to the Seminary of Kraków, and Karol continued his studies there.

That same year, Karol also became a professor at the Catholic University of Lublin, which, at the time, was the only Catholic university in the Communist world. But now Karol had to commute on the overnight train between Lublin and Kraków in order to fulfill his obligations to teach and counsel students in one city and to study in the other.

Karol also founded and ran a marriage institute that dealt with various marital problems, from family planning and illegitimacy, to alcoholism and physical abuse.

In 1956, Karol was named to the position of Chair of Ethics at the Catholic University of Lublin, and in 1958, he was named auxiliary bishop to Archbishop Mons. Eugeniusz Baziak of Kraków. His ascent through the hierarchy of the Catholic Church had now begun in earnest.

In 1962, the Second Vatican Council began deliberations that would revolutionize the church. Karol was one of its leaders. The purpose of the council was to renew the spirit of the church and to reconsider its place in the modern world. One of the major changes was the replacement of the traditional language of Mass, Latin, with whatever language the people used outside of church.

That same year, upon the death of Archbishop Baziak, Karol was named vicar capitular, which meant he was the acting archbishop of Kraków.

Karol's outward personality, which had been so evident to everyone in Wadowice, now began to attract the attention of people around the world. He was considered a genial and charming companion, a good listener, but not above good-natured kidding. Several journalists, writing in international publications, called him a brilliant man, very intelligent, and very holy.

Karol was also shrewd enough not to let his distaste for Poland's Communist government show. When he was named as cardinal in 1967 by Pope Paul VI, the government welcomed the move. Although many Communist officials considered Karol tough, they also thought he was flexible and would be moderate in his reforms. He was certainly an improvement on the previous leaders of the church, who had refused to cooperate in any way with the government.

What the Polish government didn't realize, though, was that Karol was simply biding his time, engaging in a strategy that would honor Catholic beliefs and traditions while at the same time accommodating the Communists.

In Poland, the Catholic Church had always been an outlet for the expression of national feeling, and the government officials knew enough to leave it alone. It was to Karol's credit that he encouraged religious expression by the people in a form that did not provoke brutal reactions from the state police. At the same time, though, as an enemy of Communism and a champion of human rights, Karol, through his powerful preaching and his sophisticated intellect, was able to accomplish his own agenda. He demanded permits to build churches, he defended youth groups wanting to meet for religious purposes, and he ordained priests to work underground against the Communist government of Czechoslovakia.

When asked if he feared retribution from Polish government officials, Karol replied, "I'm not afraid of them. They are afraid of me."

Although his priestly duties took up most of his time, Karol still continued his scholarly activities and published several influential works, including *Love and Responsibility*, which laid out the foundation for a modern Catholic sexual ethic.

Although Karol was known within the Catholic Church as a formidable intellectual and an able administrator and fund-raiser, very few people thought that the Sacred College of Cardinals would choose him as the next pope after the death of John Paul I in September 1978.

After seven rounds of balloting, though, when the cardinals were unable to agree on a candidate, Karol was chosen on the eighth round late in the afternoon of October 16. He was the first Slavic pope in history and the first non-Italian pope in 455 years. At age fifty-eight, Karol was also the youngest pope in 132 years.

With tears in his eyes, Karol formally accepted his election. In keeping with the tradition of popes not using their real names, Karol added another Roman numeral and became Pope John Paul II, having chosen the same name as his predecessor, whose reign had lasted just thirty-four days before he died of a heart attack.

From the balcony overlooking St. Peter's Square in Rome, Karol told his first audience, "I was afraid to receive this nomination, but I did it in the spirit of obedience to Our Lord and in the total confidence in His mother, the most Holy Madonna."

In Moscow, when Yuri Andropov, the leader

of the Soviet Union's much-feared KGB intelligence agency, learned of Karol's election as pope, he warned the government that there could be trouble ahead. He was proven correct.

CHAPTER FOURTEEN
THE PAPAL YEARS

A week after his 1978 inauguration, Karol returned to Poland as Pope John Paul II. He was there for nine days.

Wherever the pope went, he was met by huge, adoring crowds, but his visit was also a source of embarrassment to the Communist government, because Poland was supposed to be atheistic, which meant the official policy of the country was that God didn't exist. Fortunately, the government was wise enough not to press that issue too much, because the pope, as a son of Poland, was so well loved.

At the time, though, Poland was also suffering from serious food shortages, but the people had simply accepted this as their lot in life and had not protested to the government about it.

In talking to the crowds about their rights as human beings, the pope said, "You are men and women. You have dignity. Don't crawl on your bellies before anyone."

Many people believe that this was the beginning of the end of Communism in Europe.

In 1981, a Turk named Mehmet Ali Agca shot the pope twice in an assassination attempt. At first, Agca told the authorities that he was acting at the request of the Bulgarian intelligence service. Since the Bulgarians were known to do the bidding of the Soviet KGB, Agca's story was believed. It was common knowledge that the KGB wanted to get rid of the pope because of his opposition to Communism. Later, though, Agca recanted that part of his confession. When the pope visited Agca in his cell to forgive him for what he had tried to do, the would-be assassin was astonished.

Unlike many popes before him, John Paul II knew how to work a crowd. His moves, his presence, his smile, his friendliness, and his gestures pleased everyone. He shook hands, he made small talk, and he kissed babies.

While other popes had preferred to stay close to Rome, remaining remote and unapproachable, John Paul traveled widely, making 179 visits to over 115 countries, all in the first twenty years of his papacy. He was the most traveled pope in history. He spoke eight languages, having learned Spanish after he became pope. Because of his sense of theater, coming from spending years as an actor, John Paul was always quick to use the media and technology to his advantage.

In 1997, when the pope returned to Poland, the crowds, at his appearance, grew silent. Awestruck, some people fell to their knees and wept as he parted the throng on his way to the altar. According to CNN's 1999 special report on Pope John Paul II, the mayor of Nowej Soli, Krzysztof Gonet, said, "It was an incredible moment. You could feel the vibrations in the air."

In the winter of 1999, the pope flew to Mexico and the United States. Wherever he stopped—Mexico City, Boston, New York City, Philadelphia, Des Moines, Chicago, and Washington, to name a few cities—he was welcomed with opened arms, and his visit became a reason to celebrate. He held Mass for millions of people, Catholics and non-Catholics alike. Journalists called the throngs staggering and the events unprecedented.

By January 2001, it was obvious to most observers that the Pope's health was slowly deteriorating. One of his doctors finally announced publicly that John Paul was suffering from Parkinson's disease. Although the pope had shown symptoms of shaking and a general unsteadiness for several years, the Vatican had never officially acknowledged that John Paul had the disease.

Not content with just tending to church affairs, the pope tried to awaken the entire world to the dignity and responsibility of defending human rights.

John Paul's criticism of dictators responsible for crimes against humanity, such as Alfredo Stroessner in Paraguay, Augusto Pinochet in Chile, and Ferdinand Marcos in the Philippines, helped encourage government opposition movements that eventually brought down those regimes. The pope was also instrumental in the downfall of Communism in Poland.

The West also received its share of criticism from the pope, as he didn't play favorites when it came to the dignity of human beings. He suggested that wealthy nations lower their standard of living and share their wealth with the people who live in poorer countries.

Unfortunately, this criticism fell on deaf ears, but that didn't stop the pope from insisting that materialism—*owning* lots of things, such as automobiles, big houses, and expensive clothes—was not the answer to the world's problems.

According to the pope, the world was not capable of making people happy. Only prayer and faith could do that, he believed, and he tried to lead by example. He was so often in prayer that people often said he made his decisions "on his knees."

When Karol became pope in 1978, the Catholic Church was in shambles. The reforms that had begun with the Second Vatican Council had shaken the church's foundation. Many people compared it to the turmoil the United States had faced during the 1960s, with its racial strife and protests over the war in Vietnam. During this time, the church lost one third of its priests and a large number of its nuns.

Karol began a total restoration of the church, one grounded in its conservative tradition. His rejection of both contraception and abortion was absolute. When his critics called his decisions dictatorial, he replied by saying, "It's a mistake to apply American democratic procedures to faith and truth. You cannot take a vote on the truth." Such comments gave rise to the criticism that Pope John Paul

II, while charming, was closed-minded.

The pope received more criticism when he said that most of the industrialized nations of the world were fostering a culture of death because of their support of contraception, abortion, and, in some countries, euthanasia.

The pope's position on the role of women in the church was another source of conflict. He insisted that church doctrine prohibited women from becoming priests. He affirmed this position in a letter to bishops, saying, "This judgment is to be definitively held by all the church's faithful."

Although the church expanded in Africa and Latin America—the latter of which accounts for about half of the estimated one billion Catholics—during John Paul's reign as pope, it lost followers in the industrialized world, including Poland, because of his conservative rulings. This led many church observers to see John Paul's record as pope as a mixed one.

Still, most people agreed—some grudgingly—that this was a pope who did not look at the public opinion polls, who said what he thought was right or wrong out of conviction, and who was admired even by people with opposite views as a man of integrity and prayer.

CHAPTER FIFTEEN

THE LAST DAYS OF POPE JOHN PAUL II

On February 1, 2005, Pope John Paul II was rushed to Rome's Gemelli Polyclinic Hospital suffering from breathing difficulties and a throat inflamed from battling the flu. A few days later, the pope returned to the Vatican, but on February 24, he was hospitalized once again. His doctors were forced to perform a tracheotomy to help him breathe. When John Paul finally returned to the Vatican on March 13, it was now evident to everyone that he would not live much longer. People all around the world began to follow the Vatican's daily bulletins in their newspapers, on television, and on the Internet.

★ ★ ★ ★

Wednesday, March 23, 2005: Looking gaunt, the pope appears at his open studio window and blesses the faithful gathered in St. Peter's Square. In the one-minute-long appearance, the ailing pontiff raises his hand in blessing a few times but doesn't speak.

Friday, March 25, 2005: The pope uses a video connection to participate in the Way of the Cross procession at the Colosseum to mark Jesus' Crucifixion and death.

Saturday, March 26, 2005: The pope rests in his apartment so he will be ready for Easter Sunday, when he is expected to address Roman Catholics publicly for the first time in two weeks.

Sunday, March 27, 2005: The pope blesses tens of thousands of pilgrims and tourists who pack St. Peter's Square for Easter Sunday by making the sign of the cross with his hand, but he is unable to speak.

Monday, March 28, 2005: The pope skips his traditional appearance at his window overlooking St. Peter's Square the day after Easter.

Wednesday, March 30, 2005: The pope receives medical care at the Vatican. Asked about reports of a possible hospitalization, a Vatican spokesman says there are no plans at this time and that any decision will be up to the pope's doctors.

Thursday, March 31, 2005: All roads to the Vatican are closed as the health of the pope takes another downturn. The Roman Catholic sacrament for the gravely ill and the dying is administered.

Friday, April 1, 2005: Poles pack churches to pray for the recovery of the pope, after the health of the nation's most famous son takes a dramatic turn for the worse.

Friday, April 1, 2005: The Vatican announces that the pope is deteriorating again. He loses consciousness just after sunset in Rome. A large Mass is held for him there.

Saturday, April 2, 2005: Pilgrims and tourists begin filling St. Peter's Square to keep vigil as the pope nears death.

Saturday, April 2, 2005: The Vatican announces the pope's death in an e-mail: The Holy Father died this evening at 9:37 p.m. [Italian time] in his private apartment.

Sunday, April 3, 2005: Dignitaries, associates, and friends of the pope gather at the Vatican to pay their respects at the Apostolic Palace, where the Pope's body is on display.

Monday, April 4, 2005: The pope's body lies in state for viewing by the public in the Papal Palace in Castel Gandolfo.

Friday, April 8, 2005: A funeral Mass is said for the pope at St. Peter's Basilica. It is attended by dignitaries from around the world.

Monday, April 18, 2005: The College of Cardinals gathers in Rome to elect a new pope.

April 19, 2005: The College of Cardinals selects Cardinal Joseph Ratzinger of Germany to be the 265th pope of the Roman Catholic Church. He will be known as Pope Benedict XVI.

FOR MORE INFORMATION

BOOKS

Allegri, Renzo; Marsha Daigle-Williamson,
  translator.
  John Paul II: A Life of Grace.
  Cincinnati: St. Anthony Messenger Press,
  2005.

Bernstein, Carl, and Marco Politi.
  *His Holiness: John Paul II and the Hidden
  History of Our Time.*
  New York: Doubleday, 1996.

Kwitny, Jonathan.
  *Man of the Century: The Life and Times of
  Pope John Paul II.*
  New York: Henry Holt and Company, 1997.

Weigel, George.
  *Witness to Hope: The Biography of Pope John
  Paul II.*
  New York: Cliff Street Books/HarperCollins,
  2001.

WEB SITE

http://www.vatican.va
  This is the official Web site of the Holy See.

CHILDHOOD OF WORLD FIGURES

CHRISTOPHER COLUMBUS

ANNE FRANK

DIANA, PRINCESS OF WALES

COMING SOON:

LEONARDO DA VINCI

★　★ COLLECT THEM ALL! ★　★